IN AN AGE OF
COHABITATION

How and When People Tie the Knot
in the Twenty-First Century

Maureen Baker & Vivienne Elizabeth

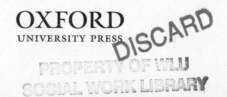

OXFORD
UNIVERSITY PRESS

OXFORD
UNIVERSITY PRESS

Oxford University Press is a department of the University of Oxford.
It furthers the University's objective of excellence in research, scholarship,
and education by publishing worldwide. Oxford is a registered trade mark of
Oxford University Press in the UK and in certain other countries.

Published in Canada by
Oxford University Press
8 Sampson Mews, Suite 204,
Don Mills, Ontario M3C 0H5 Canada

www.oupcanada.com

Library and Archives Canada Cataloguing in Publication

Baker, Maureen, author
Marriage in an age of cohabitation : how and when people
tie the knot in the twenty-first century / Maureen Baker and Vivienne Elizabeth.

Includes bibliographical references and index.
ISBN 978-0-19-900263-4 (pbk.)

1. Marriage. 2. Unmarried couples. 3. Domestic relations.
I. Elizabeth, Vivienne author II. Title.

HQ734.B22 2014   306.81   C2013-906132-0

Printed and bound in the United States of America.

1 2 3 4 — 17 16 15 14

Contents

Acknowledgements

This book began in 2008 as a joint research project called "Negotiating the Transition from Cohabitation to Marriage/Civil Union." The Faculty of Arts at the University of Auckland provided funding for this research, which enabled us to hire a post-graduate student to help review previous research (Rachel Stiff), four students to help interview participants (Laila Behmeleit, Merita Muaulu Sailii, Jo Buckton, and Kat Forbes), and a transcriber (Jan Rhodes) to convert the recorded interviews into written transcripts. We would like to acknowledge the contribution these women made to the completion of the research behind the book.

In addition, we would like to thank the ten celebrants who served as "key informants" for the project and gave their time and expertise to discuss why cohabiting couples decide to marry and the kinds of ceremonies they have presided over. We would also like to thank the forty cohabitants who generously provided their personal stories about how and why they eventually made the transition from cohabitation to marriage or civil union. The findings from these forty interviews were analyzed and compared with the results of previous studies to form the backbone of this book.

We would also like to thank the Department of Sociology for providing conference funding, enabling us to present our findings to overseas colleagues, and to express our appreciation for the opportunity to discuss this research and its implications with colleagues and our partners. Finally we would like to thank Katie Scott and her colleagues at Oxford University Press in Toronto for managing our manuscript from the reviewing stage to its final publication.

CHAPTER 1

The Rise of Do-It-Yourself (DIY) "Marriage"

Introduction

For decades, sociologists have debated whether widespread hetero-sexual cohabitation represents a new lifestyle choice that weakens the social institution of marriage, or whether it simply indicates a delayed pathway to more conventional legal relationships.[1] The recent visibility of same-sex cohabitation and the legal recognition of these partnerships in many parts of the developed world have also led to vigorous debates about the changing nature of intimate relationships and the meaning of marriage.

If consensual unions or "DIY marriage" (Duncan et al. 2005) represent a weakening of marriage, why do so many different-sex couples who live together eventually formalize their relationships? If cohabitation is the preferred pathway to marriage, civil union/partnerships, or remarriage, why do different-sex cohabiting couples postpone their weddings for such a long time, and what do they hope to gain from formalizing their relationships? Why do same-sex couples who cohabit vacillate over whether or not to take advantage of their hard-won rights to legally partner? Why do some long-term different-sex cohabitants grandly announce their "engagement" to family and friends, expecting them to congratulate them and celebrate their decision when they have lived together for years? After all, some of these newly engaged couples have already

---

1. Cohabitation is also referred to as consensual unions, common-law relationships, de-facto unions, and DIY or do-it-yourself marriage.

bought houses together and started raising children, which presumably entails some level of commitment.

This book discusses the reasons why individuals and couples who previously cohabited choose to formalize their long-term intimate relationships. While there are still some legal and social advantages to be gained from marriage, these are less obvious for different-sex couples than for same-sex couples, who in many jurisdictions are still struggling to gain full social and legal recognition of their relationships. This book also explores the decision-making processes surrounding the transition to cohabitation and "marriage" and how couples actually decide to solemnize and celebrate what is for many a significant life event. We investigate the meanings that "marriage" has for different-sex and same-sex couples at varying stages of their lives and in different jurisdictions.

We are particularly interested in the negotiation processes between partners, whether the decision to legalize initially came from one or the other party or was the result of mutual discussion, and what the decision to marry actually means to each of them and to their associates. Do same-sex couples and older couples who are already parents and/or grandparents decide to legalize their relationships in the same way and for similar reasons? Do heterosexual men still propose marriage to women? Who proposes in same-sex couples? And what impact does prior cohabitation or marriage have on the style and average cost of weddings? We draw on a wide range of international studies and statistics on cohabitation and marriage in this book, focusing mainly on research from Canada and the English-speaking countries of Australia, New Zealand, the United Kingdom, and the United States of America. We also include the findings from our qualitative interviews in New Zealand with marriage and civil-union celebrants, and long-term cohabitants who had decided to marry or enter a civil union or had already done so.

Previous studies and our own interviews show that both different-sex and same-sex couples increasingly delay their weddings until they have experienced several years of successful cohabitation and achieved significant material goals, including saving up enough money for what they are encouraged to see as a "proper" wedding. Where legally possible, many couples in the twenty-first century personalize their ceremony and reception with promises, songs/ poems, outfits, and decorations that have special meaning for them as a couple. However, regardless of their sexual orientation or personal beliefs, many couples also retain traditional wedding practices that used to symbolize patriarchy and heterosexuality. In addition, some couples plan elaborate and expensive events even when they have access to limited financial resources, although others stitch together more modest occasions with the help of family and friends.

In this book we initially place quotation marks around such words as "engagement," "wedding," and "marriage" to indicate that although these words have been traditionally associated with transition points for different-sex couples, they are increasingly being used to refer to similar transitions for same-sex couples. In some English-speaking countries (such as Australia and most states of the United States), same-sex couples are still not able to marry but they may be able to legalize their relationships through civil partnerships or civil unions, which create similar possibilities for celebrating relationships and offer similar relationship rights. Canada legalized same-sex marriage in 2005 and New Zealand in April 2013, while the United Kingdom was still debating this issue at the time of writing.

The first chapter asks why most couples initially cohabit, sometimes without any clear intention of marrying in the near future, and why many eventually decide to formalize their relationship after a few years of cohabitation. We discuss these questions within the social and demographic context involving rising cohabitation rates and declining marriage rates in Canada, Australia, New Zealand, the United Kingdom, and the United States. The chapter notes the social, legal, economic, and cultural reasons for the widespread trend toward cohabitation, especially before marriage and among different-sex couples, but we also investigate the statistical differences and similarities found between cohabiting same-sex and different-sex couples and married heterosexual couples. Both the reasons behind the trends and the socio-political implications resulting from them will be explored. First, we comment on the widespread trend toward non-marital cohabitation.

The Rise of Cohabitation or Consensual Unions

In the past few decades, legal marriage rates have declined in Western industrialized countries. In 2006, for example, the crude marriage rate across twenty-six countries in the Organisation for Economic Co-operation and Development (OECD) was 5.1 per 1,000 people, more than a third less than in 1970 (OECD 2009: 68). At the same time, rates of cohabitation have increased for both different-sex and same-sex couples (OECD 2009: 69; May 2011). Rising cohabitation rates and the increased visibility of same-sex couples have contributed to popular and political anxieties about the nature of family change and its social implications, but they have also become central to sociological debates about the rise of individualism and secularization, and the "de-traditionalization" of society.

Sociologists have typically argued that widespread cohabitation shows that couples are rejecting the traditional models of intimate relationships in favour of "constructing their own biographies of love," which tend to last only as long as they are mutually beneficial (Amato et al. 2007; Beck and Beck-Gernsheim 1995; Cherlin 2010; Duncan et al. 2005; Lewis et al. 2002). British sociologist Anthony Giddens (1992: 58) coined the term *pure relationship* to refer to the emergence of intimate relationships that are entered into for their own sake and are sustained only "so far as it is thought by both parties to deliver enough satisfactions for each individual to stay within it." He particularly saw same-sex couples as trailblazers in "consensual love." Nevertheless, other researchers have concluded that marriage as a cultural ideal remains influential because it symbolizes a higher level of commitment, operates as a marker of prestige in a world of declining heterosexual marriage rates, and affords couples a sense of security in the face of anxiety arising from enhanced levels of personal choice (Cherlin 2004; Gross 2005; Lauer and Yodanis 2010; Manning et al. 2007; Sassler and Miller 2011).

Rising rates of non-marital cohabitation are important sociologically, not just because of what they suggest about contemporary intimate life, but also because they have been linked to other social and demographic changes. First, the diminishing influence of organized religion (or the secularization of society), as well as the growth of individualism, have provided both different-sex and same-sex couples with opportunities to depart from conventional social practices relating to intimate relationships and to construct and follow their own personal choices. Second, greater sexual freedom has enabled different-sex couples to explore their sexuality outside of legalized frameworks without as much fear of familial or social condemnation, while improvements in birth control have meant that sexual intimacy carries with it fewer risks of an unplanned pregnancy. Third, increasing social acceptance of same-sex relationships, together with advances in reproductive technologies, has permitted a growing number of same-sex couples to live openly together and to bear and rear children, thereby creating "families of choice" (Weston 1991).

The fourth social change linked to cohabitation is that rising rates of higher education and employment among women have reduced their reliance on marriage and husbands for financial security, which helps explain both delayed marriage and the decline in marriage rates for different-sex couples. Finally, cross-national variations in the prevalence of consensual unions suggest that both cohabitation and marriage rates are influenced by cultural values, laws, and social policies (Baker 2010; Liefbroer and Dourleijn 2006; OECD 2009: 68). For example, some jurisdictions deny certain legal rights to unmarried cohabitants and their children, or offer additional tax benefits to legally married couples to provide an incentive for heterosexual marriage. In these jurisdictions, marriage is seen by the government as the only suitable living arrangement for child-rearing and the basis of a more stable and moral society.

Prior to the 1980s, governments did not report on different-sex or same-sex cohabitation in their official statistics because such unions were socially frowned upon and the numbers were too small, which makes it difficult for researchers to compare long-term trends across different jurisdictions. Furthermore, the collection of official statistics for same-sex couples remains in its infancy, which limits the possibility of noting long-term trends in the formation, legalization, and dissolution of these relationships. Reliance on statistics that are more than a decade old is also typical of cross-national research on patterns of cohabitation, despite its rapid change and increasing prevalence (Liefbroer and Dourleijn 2006). In addition, statistics from varying sources are sometimes calculated in different ways. International figures from the Organisation for Economic Co-operation and Development (OECD) indicate that the *percentage of adults* (aged twenty and over) who are currently married, cohabiting, or in civil partnerships varies considerably by country, reflecting legal and cultural differences. Table 1 indicates the variation in cohabitation rates, with Italy showing the lowest cohabitation rate and the highest marriage rate in this table.

Cohabitation rates are also calculated as a percentage of all *couple households* or a percentage of *census families*. Canadian figures indicate that the percentage of cohabiting couples rates has

Table 1   Percentage of Adults (20 years and over) Who Are Married or Cohabiting

Country	Married	Cohabiting
Australia	51.2	8.9
Canada	39.3	8.9
Denmark	40.8	11.5
France	44.6	14.4
Italy	53.9	2.0
New Zealand	48.6	9.3
United Kingdom	47.3	8.7
United States	52.9	6.8

Source: Extracted from OECD Family Database, 2010, http://www.oecd.org/els/soc/oecdfamilydatabase.htm

increased from 6.3 percent of all couples in the early 1980s to 18.4 percent in 2006, if we combine same-sex with different-sex couples in the recent statistics (Wu 2000: 50; Statistics Canada 2007a). In 2011, "common-law" couples accounted for 16.7 percent of all census families, which represents an increase of 13.9 percent since 2006 (Statistics Canada 2012). In Quebec, the cohabitation rate is much higher than the rest of Canada, at 34.6 percent of couple households. Le Bourdais and Lapierre-Adamcyk (2004) argue that cohabitation in Quebec, as in Sweden, is nearly indistinguishable from marriage while in the rest of Canada it is still accepted predominantly as a childless phase in conjugal life, as in the other English-speaking countries.

The United Kingdom government reported that cohabitation rates increased from 9 percent of all couple families in 1996 to 15.3 percent in 2010, with most cohabiting couples under the age of forty-five years (Fairbairn 2011; UK Office of National Statistics 2010). Australian statistics show a similar trend, with cohabiting couples increasing from 4 percent of all couples in 1982 (Dempsey and de Vaus 2004) to 14.9 percent in 2006 (AIFS 2008). In addition, 78 percent of registered marriages involve couples who had previously cohabited (ibid). In the United States data from the 2002 National Survey of Family Growth indicated that cohabiting unions made up 15 percent of all unions, and 52 percent of marriages began as cohabiting unions (Kennedy and Bumpass 2008). Similar trends are also apparent in New Zealand but the statistics are presented for people fifteen to forty-four years old, where two in five men and women between these ages are living in "de-facto" unions (Statistics New Zealand 2012: 61).

In addition, more same-sex couples now live together openly, especially in larger cities, although the official numbers remain very small. In the Australian and New Zealand censuses of 2006, only 0.7 percent of all couples who reported living together were same-sex partners (Baker 2010: 60). In Canada, between 2006 and 2011 there was a slight increase in same-sex couples reporting to be living together from 0.6 percent to 0.8 percent of all couples

(Statistics Canada 2012). In the United States, 1.0 percent of couple households consisted of same-sex partners in 2010 (US Census 2011b). However, these figures include only those same-sex couples living in long-term stable relationships who reported their living arrangements to government officials.

Some individuals who regularly have gay or lesbian relationships live alone while others may identify as bisexuals and live in heterosexual marriages. American studies suggest that about 3 percent of American men and less than 2 percent of American women report that their sexual partners are exclusively of the same sex (Ambert 2005). In addition, Black et al. (2000) estimated that 30 percent of gay men and 46 percent of lesbian women had previously been married to heterosexual partners.

Official statistics tend to regard cohabiting couples in homogenous terms. However, cohabitation is a heterogeneous and fluid phenomenon for both different-sex and same-sex couples, although we know much less about the latter. It is thought that for the majority of different-sex couples, cohabitation takes the form of a *trial marriage* that allows them to see if they are suitably matched and can "justify the next step" (Carmichael and Whittaker 2007b; Coast 2009; Manning et al. 2011; Qu 2003). For these couples, cohabitation is part of the courtship process and is therefore on a pathway to marriage. Indeed, premarital cohabitation has become a normative prerequisite for marriage, with the vast majority of couples in English-speaking countries cohabiting prior to marrying. However, previous research also indicates that partners do not always agree about the wisdom of cohabiting before marriage. Those with strong religious convictions or whose friends and family disapprove of cohabitation are less likely to agree to cohabit, regardless of the wishes of their romantic partner. Furthermore, studies suggest that heterosexual women who are already cohabiting are more likely than men to view their living arrangements as a trial marriage (Dempsey and de Vaus 2004; Manning et al. 2007; Manning et al. 2011; Qu et al. 2009). It is unlikely that many same-sex couples understand their relationships as trial marriages, given their historical exclusion from marriage. However, as same-sex marriage (or other forms of legalization) becomes more customary, it may well be that same-sex couples also begin to frame cohabitation in terms of a trial marriage.

Another common pattern, especially among young people, involves cohabitation as *co-residential dating*. These relationships are very much about the here and now, without any particular thought to the future. Such a practice arises out of changes to social mores, which means that young couples can achieve the intimacy they desire through living together without facing serious or immediate pressure from family members. For different-sex couples, this pressure has historically been to legalize their relationship through marriage, but with same-sex couples the pressure has tended to take the form of opposition to their relationship unless it is kept ambiguous.

Among a smaller group of cohabiting couples, cohabitation is actively chosen as an *alternative to marriage*, either because they reject the patriarchal, heterosexual, or religious overtones associated with marriage, want to avoid its legal ramifications, or, for same-sex couples, because they have no way of legalizing their relationship (Elizabeth 1997). Finally, there are long-term, different-sex cohabitants, typically with children, for whom cohabitation is largely *indistinguishable from marriage*. Referring to the situation in Sweden, Heuveline and Timberlake (2004) suggest that the last group of cohabiting couples may simply be indifferent to legalizing their relationship because of the decreased salience of marriage as a cultural ideal, the widespread acceptance of different-sex cohabitation, and the tendency for social institutions not to differentiate between married and cohabiting different-sex couples. However, research in English-speaking countries indicates that this group of cohabitants are sometimes dealing with unplanned pregnancies, financial insecurity, or doubts about their choice of partner (Lewis 2001; Smart and Stevens 2000). Moreover, there is some evidence to suggest that increased economic security, usually in the form of higher male wages, prompts these cohabitants to convert their relationships to marriages, because at least for the women, their male partners have become "marriage worthy" (Smock and Manning 1997).

Australian researchers have found that the relationships of different-sex cohabitants tend to be newly formed, with most either converting to marriage or dissolving within less than three years of living together (Qu et al. 2009). However, demographers predict that the conversion rates for different-sex couples from cohabitation to marriage will decline over time as cohabitation becomes more socially acceptable and the legal differences diminish between marriage and cohabitation. In 2001, Statistics Canada projected that about 75 percent of those aged thirty to thirty-nine would marry at some point in their lives, but 90 percent of fifty- to sixty-nine-year-olds were already married at that time (Statistics Canada 2002b). This suggests a generational change in marriage practices, at least among different-sex couples, meaning that there could be a substantial decline in the percentage of legally married couples in the future. As legal marriage rates decline, cohabitation increases, but this living arrangement still remains more prevalent among younger couples. For example, nearly 90 percent of Australian men aged fifteen to nineteen and living with a partner were cohabiting, compared to less than 5 percent of men sixty-five and older (AIFS 2008).

When couples are seen together in public, it is not always possible to distinguish between those who are cohabiting and those who are legally married unless you gain additional personal knowledge about them (Baker 2010). Same-sex couples who are cohabiting or married often refer to their "partner" but many different-sex couples use the term *partner* interchangeably with *husband* and *wife*. Some cohabiting partners wear wedding-like rings while some married partners do not. Some married women retain their birth name while others change to their husband's surname or hyphenate both names together; only a small minority of same-sex partners change their surnames when they legalize their relationships. Some cohabiting couples share bank accounts while some married couples keep their money in separate accounts. Despite this degree of overlap, researchers have found statistical differences between different-sex cohabiting and married couples.

Research from various English-speaking countries reveals that different-sex cohabitants tend to be younger than married partners, have fewer children, have lower incomes, are less religious and less conventional, and are more likely to have been previously married and divorced (Daly and Rake 2003; Duncan et al. 2005; Lichter et al. 2006; Qu and Weston 2008a; Wilson 2009; Wu 2000). Researchers have also found differences relating to gender roles and social attitudes among different-sex couples. For example, women in cohabiting relationships are more likely than married women to be employed full-time, to have fewer or no children, and to expect an egalitarian division of labour (Baxter 2002). Several studies, such as Baxter et al. (2010) and Davis et al. (2007) also showed that cohabiting men do slightly more housework than married men, while cohabiting women do less housework than their married counterparts. American research has found that women are less likely than men to be involved in multiple cohabitations and that different-sex "serial cohabiters" are over-represented among disadvantaged groups, especially those with low income and education (Lichter and Qian 2008).

Many of the characteristics of different-sex couples who live together—their relative young age and lower incomes, their tendency to be childless, their comparative unconventionality and lower levels of religiosity—are also associated with relationship instability. Given that cohabitation for many different-sex couples might better be understood as trial marriage or co-residential dating, it is not surprising that cohabiting couples experience higher rates of separation than married partners. Statistics Canada reports that first common-law relationships or consensual unions are twice as likely to end in separation as first marriages but also that first unions among younger couples are more likely to end in separation than those among older couples regardless of their marital status (Statistics Canada 2002). Australian data indicates that cohabiting relationships are three times more likely than legally married relationships to end in separation (Qu and Weston 2008b).

Studies from several countries suggest that the statistical differences between different-sex cohabitants and married couples are diminishing as a larger percentage of the population cohabits (de Vaus, Qu, and Weston 2005; Liefbroer and Dourleijn 2006). Others caution against the tendency to commit the "statistical error of not comparing like with like" (Duncan, Barlow, and James 2005; Smart 2011). It is not that cohabitation is the source of relationship instability, but rather that other socio-economic differences between cohabiting and married couples mean that cohabiting relationships are less stable.

Researchers predict that as cohabitation becomes more prevalent, the differences between heterosexual cohabiting and married couples will decline even further. Over three-quarters of couples now cohabit before marriage in the English-speaking countries and much of Western Europe, and some of these statistical differences (such as in age and income) are already showing signs of diminishing (Baker 2010; Hewitt and de Vaus 2009; Pongracz and Spéder 2008; Statistics New Zealand 2010b). In addition, we might expect that the longer cohabiting couples remain together, the more likely they will be viewed by others (and perhaps by themselves) as similar to married couples.

A number of studies find that gay and lesbian couples do not differ significantly from different-sex couples, although there are some notable exceptions (Ambert 2005). Some researchers have found that same-sex couples tend to display less allegiance to monogamy and permanent relationships, and less conventionality in sexual identity than married different-sex couples (Ambert 2005; Sarantakos 1998). However, gay men typically display less commitment to monogamy than either lesbians or heterosexual couples, and cohabiting different-sex partners show less commitment to monogamy than married different-sex partners.

Researchers have also found that gay and lesbian couples reported more autonomy in their activities, friendships, and decision-making than heterosexual married couples (Kurdeck 1998, 2001; Weeks 2002). They also report less approval of their relationships from their birth families, lower levels of commitment between partners, and higher rates of relationship dissolution than heterosexual couples. However, cohabiting same-sex couples have also been viewed as trailblazers because they tend to report a more egalitarian division of labour in the home than married different-sex couples (Giddens 1992; Dunne 1997; Patterson 2000; Shechory and Ziv 2007; Solomon et al. 2005). In addition, researchers from a number of countries have found that same-sex partners who legalize their relationships tend to be older than different-sex couples who marry (Einarsdottir 2011).

Notwithstanding these similarities and differences, same-sex couples have historically been denied legal recognition of their relationships. Some same-sex couples have been and remain happy to share a home without any legal recognition, even though this could influence their acknowledgement as next of kin and deny them the privileges that accompany marriage, such as visiting rights if one partner should be admitted to a hospital. Moreover, should they be parenting a child together, the non-biological partner may not be seen as a legitimate parent or guardian by school officials, doctors, or immigration officers. In many countries, same-sex couples have fought for greater respect for their relationships and legal recognition, including relationship rights or public acknowledgement as a "spouse" or partner, permission to marry, and equal access to assisted reproduction services, child-fostering, and adoption (Ambert 2005; Baker 2010; McNair et al. 2002; Weeks 2002). The legalization of same-sex relationships, discussed in more detail later in this chapter, remains controversial and continues to generate strong opposition from social and religious conservatives.

Does Cohabitation Represent a Lower Level of Relationship Commitment?

Researchers have suggested that for young different-sex couples in particular, cohabitation normally takes one of two forms: either trial marriage or co-residential dating. While the former implies at least some shared commitment to a possible future together, the latter leaves the question of a commitment to a future together open. As Lindsay (2000) found in her Australian study, many young heterosexual couples offered pragmatic reasons for moving in together, often constructing cohabitation as a matter of mere convenience rather than an indicator of increased interpersonal commitment. The ambiguity that surrounded the meaning of cohabitation was matched by an ambiguity in the level of commitment; the different-sex couples in Lindsay's study seldom talked about marriage because they needed to see how their relationship developed.

In an American study, Stanley et al. (2006) observed that many different-sex couples "slide" from dating to cohabitation in a non-deliberative and incremental way, without fully considering all the implications. However, as cohabiting couples entwined their lives together through the joint purchase of household goods and jointly signed rental agreements, they increased the obstacles to their separation, a process that generated what they called "relationship inertia." Stanley and colleagues concluded that compared to dating, cohabitation not only encourages couples to remain in relationships that may not be fully satisfying yet are more complex to end, but it also facilitates a "slide" into marriages that are less rewarding and more at risk of dissolution. Significantly, they point out that the process of sliding rather than deciding is linked to gender differences in levels of interpersonal commitment among cohabiting couples and those who cohabited prior to marriage. They found that men typically report substantially lower levels of commitment than women in both relational settings.

Contradictory evidence about the question of commitment among different-sex cohabiting couples has emerged from several other studies. Lewis (1999) found that cohabiting and married parents in the United Kingdom said that they had already made private commitments to each other and to their children. The younger generation of parents talked about commitments as personal issues that were internally driven, whereas their own parents talked more about obligations that were externally imposed and commitments that were made in public. Jamieson et al. (2002) found that legal marriage was seen as irrelevant to commitment by many Scottish young people who were twenty to twenty-nine years old, although some saw legal marriage as important for child-rearing.

Studies about cohabitation and commitment sometimes find that couples *say* that they are committed to their partners, yet statistically their relationships are more likely than marriages to end in separation. As we have observed above, this could be a result of socio-economic and age differences between cohabiting and married couples. However, it could also indicate that a legally binding public commitment which is witnessed by friends and family is more likely to last than a private commitment made as a couple. One of the reasons for this distinction is that public commitments enhance the level of what Rhoades, Stanley, and Markman (2010) call "constraint commitment." Constraint commitment refers to barriers to leaving a relationship and includes such factors as the presence of children, a belief in the sanctity of relationships, a perception that one would be worse off outside of the relationship, social pressures to stay together, investments in jointly owned property, and the difficulty of obtaining a divorce or breaking up.

The public nature of marriage commitments means that the end of the relationship is inevitably, in some shape or form, public too. For instance, the marital status of formerly married individuals changes to "separated" or "divorced," whereas the marital status of formerly cohabiting individuals remains "single." This raises the possibility that formerly married couples, but not formerly cohabiting couples, will often be reminded of the failure of their relationships. In some instances, they may be stigmatized by the revelation of their marital status, a fate less likely to befall former cohabiting couples.

The social and legal context is clearly changing to enable couples to experience intimacy, even to buy houses and raise children together, but to delay formalizing their commitment to each other through legal marriage. The next section will discuss some of these societal changes in more detail.

The Changing Social Context of Intimate Relationships

Cohabitation is typically a temporary state. Although a few couples choose to retain their informal status and cohabit for a lifetime, most couples either formalize their relationships or separate. A central question of this book is, why do so many of the cohabiting couples who decide to stay together eventually legalize their relationships? Of course, the answer to this question may well turn out to be dissimilar for different-sex and same-sex couples, since the former have historically been subject to pressure to marry, while the latter have historically been barred from marrying (Shipman and Smart 2007). In addition, the book asks, why do some cohabiting couples who initially viewed marriage or civil union as unnecessary or overly conventional subsequently later decide to marry, and then organize events that retain many of the symbols of traditional and patriarchal weddings? We begin to answer these questions by discussing the changing socio-legal context of intimate relationships. We consider the changes that have taken place in different-sex relationships before turning to discuss those that have influenced same-sex couples.

Different-Sex Couples Delay Marriage but Not Sexual Activity

The decline in legal marriage rates among different-sex couples since the 1970s is attributed both to the rise in informal living arrangements and the reduced relevance of marriage as a form of financial security for women. Marriage rates have declined at varying rates in different countries, but have also created noticeable differences between generations and income groups, with older and wealthier different-sex couples much more likely to marry. Marriage rates also fluctuate with the rise and fall in living costs, especially the availability and cost of residential housing, as well as the pressures of war, employment opportunities, and the availability of contraception. In general, marriage rates reached a low point during the

Great Depression of the 1930s because couples could not afford to marry and establish separate households, but the rates rose during World War II when couples had more money and wanted to cement their unions to gain emotional security, sexual freedom, and possibly state income support if the husband was injured or killed (Baker 2010). After the war, marriage rates typically increased until the early 1970s and then have continued to fall until the present.

In the OECD countries, the average age of first marriage for different-sex couples has increased notably since the 1970s, influenced by rising educational requirements for employment, rising rates of cohabitation, and higher housing costs. In Canada, for example, the average age of first marriage in the 1960s was 22 years for women and 25 years for men, but this increased to 29.1 for women and 31.1 for men by 2008 (Statistics Canada 2007a; Vanier Institute of the Family 2011). Similar trends are apparent in the other English-speaking countries. For example, in New Zealand, the average age at first marriage in 1971 was 20.8 for brides and 23.0 for grooms, but this has increased to 28.1 and 29.8 in 2009 (Statistics New Zealand 2001, 2010a). In the United States, the age of first marriage increased from to 20.8 for women and 22.3 for men in 1970 to 26.1 and 28.2 in 2010 (US Bureau of the Census 2011a). While the average age of first marriage has increased in all the English-speaking countries, these figures show that minor variations are apparent by country. Furthermore, men continue to marry at an older average age than women.

Despite the fact that most heterosexual adults marry in their late twenties or early thirties, the average age of first sexual experience has remained relatively stable for the past few decades, at about seventeen or eighteen years of age (Nayak and Kehily 2008; Richters and Rissel 2005). This suggests that many people are sexually active well before they marry, which has been facilitated by more liberal attitudes about sexuality, improvements in birth control, and the legalization of abortion. Despite this sexual activity, women are bearing their first child later in life, at an average age of 27.7 in OECD countries in 2005 compared to 24.0 in 1970 (OECD 2009: 65). The growing tendency to postpone marriage and pregnancy provides advantages for heterosexual women, who can complete their education, find employment, and possibly become eligible for parental leave benefits before marriage and motherhood. Delayed marriage enables heterosexual men to continue their education and find better-paying jobs before becoming a household earner and father.

Voluntary Child-bearing

Historically, marriage for different-sex couples has been associated with having and raising children. Churches have traditionally viewed child-bearing as the main purpose of marriage, and after a wedding ceremony, friends and family symbolized this expectation by throwing symbols of fertility (such as confetti or rice) on the couple. It is the association between marriage and child-bearing that frequently forms the basis of religious and social conservative opposition to same-sex marriage, because they argue that same-sex couples cannot bear children together, an argument that ignores the child-bearing possibilities afforded to same-sex couples by reproductive technologies.

Although most different-sex couples and an increasing number of same-sex couples continue to bear and rear children, couples are more likely than in the past to question whether or not they really want children, when they should start trying to conceive, and how many children they should have (VIF 2008). Sociologists have argued that child-bearing for different-sex couples is still perceived as sign of maturity, normality, and sexual competence, although younger people tend to view voluntary childlessness more liberally (Baker 2010). Nevertheless, it is still widely expected that married different-sex couples *will* produce children.

The social pressure on different-sex couples to reproduce comes from many sources, including government officials, religious leaders, family, friends, and even strangers (Baker 2010). Governments and community leaders continue to see children as necessary because they will become the future generation of taxpayers, voters, workers, and consumers. Parents often want grandchildren to amuse them and later watch over them in old age, and siblings want nieces and nephews to expand their family networks (ibid). Parents also expect to share with friends their stories about the joys and challenges of child-rearing. Television advertisements show happy parents (usually mothers) interacting with healthy, smiling, and loving children. Although these advertisements are designed to encourage viewers to buy more of the advertised product, they also encourage us to see child-rearing as desirable and rewarding.

The institutional framework for child-bearing has also changed dramatically, with births outside of marriage now commonplace in many countries. However, most of these births are to cohabiting women between twenty-five and thirty-five years old (OECD 2007). Figures from the OECD reveal that an average of 28 percent of births fall outside legal marriage in these countries, and in the Nordic countries, France, Great Britain, and New Zealand, over 50 percent (OECD 2009: 65). Statistics Canada figures show that 38 percent of live births in 2006 were to women who were not married or living with their legal spouse (Statistics Canada 2008), compared to 9 percent in 1975 and 4 percent in 1960 (VIF 1994, 2000). In Australia, 33 percent of births in 2007 were to parents who were not in a registered marriage (ABS 2008).

For different-sex couples, child-bearing continues to serve as a rite of passage or a socially acknowledged transition from childhood to adulthood, and fulfills dominant conceptions of masculinity and femininity. Despite the cost of raising children and the loss of personal freedom that parents experience, many people highlight the social and psychological rewards of married parenthood and believe that it is superior to a childless marriage. As we will see later in this book, getting legally married is often viewed by different-sex couples as a step toward child-bearing and child-rearing, and cohabiting different-sex couples who plan to remain child free are less likely to marry (Qu et al. 2009).

Barriers to Legal Marriage for Different-Sex Couples

Researchers have found that different-sex couples with higher educational qualifications, steady jobs, and secure incomes have much higher marriage rates than those who are poorer, less-educated, or living in high-unemployment areas with expensive housing. As British sociologist Jane Lewis (2001: 39) noted, marriage is "practised most often by those with something to transact." Heterosexual individuals with low income and low educational attainment are only half as likely to marry but more often cohabit, and when they do marry, their divorce rates tend to be higher (McLaughlin and Lichter 1997). Economic and labour market problems seem to add stress to intimate relationships and contribute to higher rates of separation (Booth and Crouter 2002; Daly and Rake 2003). These findings are relevant to the English-speaking countries or liberal states as well as to Europe and the former communist countries (Edin and Reed 2005; Pongracz and Spéder 2008).

Social conservatives sometimes see different-sex marriage as one of the solutions to the high poverty rates in one-parent households, especially those led by sole mothers living on social benefits or low earnings. In the United States, policy-makers have suggested that sole mothers would be better off if they simply married their male partner, because this would make him responsible for supporting the entire household. Welfare programs that provide incentives such as tax advantages for cohabiting couples to marry have been jokingly labelled "wedfare." However, researchers have identified a number of barriers to marriage among those with low incomes and low levels of education.

Reviewing previous research, Edin and Reed (2005) found that materially disadvantaged men and women (those with low income and low assets) often value marriage highly and view it as "sacred," more committed than cohabitation, and something they want to do "some day." However, the ideal of marriage remains unrealized because of the complexities of their lives. Their relationships are often conflict-ridden and involve partner violence and frequent separations. Both men and women struggle to find employment that can pay the bills, and many couples experience bouts of unemployment and low-paid jobs. Before they can marry, many low-income women feel that they need a secure income, enough money for a down-payment on a modest home, some furniture, a car, some savings in the bank, and some money for a "decent" wedding (Edin and Kefalas 2005). This research suggests that material circumstances may be more influential than values in determining couples' decisions about legalization (Lewis 2001: 39).

Research in America and the United Kingdom suggests that low-income men and women no longer view marriage as a prerequisite for child-bearing, but they often say that children are better off when raised within marriage (Edin and Reed 2005; Jamieson et al. 2002). For this group, the stigma of divorce is deemed greater than the stigma of having a child outside marriage. Births outside marriage have been rising steadily in many countries for over fifty years. Wu (2008) estimates that among women born in the United States between 1965 and 1969, 20 percent of white women, 33 percent of Hispanic women and 60 percent of black women will have had a child outside formal marriage by their thirtieth birthday.

Legal marriage for different-sex couples seems to have lost some of its instrumental value as more women become self-supporting, contraception and abortion are widely available, premarital sex and cohabitation have become more socially acceptable, and marriage is no longer necessary for women's social or legal status (Edin and Reed 2005). Yet marriage remains a symbol of status and luxury. As such, it has become a relationship that carries much higher expectations of relationship quality and financial stability than cohabitation, and the majority of those who are materially disadvantaged cannot meet this higher marital standard (Cherlin 2004; Edin and Kefalas 2005). Although this reflects the realities for many different-sex individuals and couples, the situation varies somewhat for same-sex couples, as we discuss later in this chapter.

Legal Regulation: Making Different-Sex Cohabitation More Like Marriage

Policy-makers have responded to the rise in different-sex cohabitation in a variety of ways. Some jurisdictions, especially in Scandinavia, Western Europe, and much of the English-speaking world, have decided that after a certain period of time, these relationships should be considered to be similar to legal marriage in terms of spousal entitlements and obligations (Wu 2000). One entitlement that is typically granted to different-sex cohabiting couples is visiting rights or decision-making powers if the partner is in an accident or admitted to a hospital, while another is automatic eligibility as a beneficiary to the partner's health insurance plan or retirement benefits. Such rights and entitlements have been much less forthcoming for same-sex cohabiting couples, which is a key reason for calls for the legal recognition of same-sex partnerships.

Most English-speaking jurisdictions continue to withhold "next of kin" status from cohabiting partners, irrespective of their sexual orientation, making this one of the few remaining legal distinctions between cohabitation and marriage (Bainham 2006). New Zealand has moved further than most jurisdictions in conferring rights and responsibilities to cohabitants that historically have been attached to formal relationship status. In most instances where marriages or civil unions are recognized as having legal consequences, so too is long-term cohabitation (Inglis 2007).

Many jurisdictions have made similar decisions about shared assets and how they should normally be divided if the couple should separate. In many English-speaking jurisdictions, legal reforms already require the equal division of family assets when marriage partners separate, unless doing so would create inequity or unfairness. This rule has been extended to different-sex cohabiting couples in countries such as Canada and New Zealand, although not the United Kingdom and some American or Australian states. In some jurisdictions, such as Canada and New Zealand, this rule has also been extended to same-sex cohabiting couples. Like married spouses, cohabiting partners in Canada and New Zealand who do not wish to divide their property equally if they separate in the future must sign a legal contract to specify alternative arrangements. However, all jurisdictions agree that parents must support any children they produce, whether or not parents are legally married or living with their children. Increasingly, governments and social agencies disregard legal marital status in their treatment of different-sex couples, families, and children, and these policies and practices tend to make marriage or civil union even less relevant, at least in legal terms (Heuveline and Timberlake 2004).

Other jurisdictions, such as the United Kingdom, have maintained the distinction between cohabiting and married couples, partly because they see marriage as a "sacrament" and/or legal contract, but also because not all cohabiting couples want more legal rights and obligations. Some cohabitants see no practical advantage to formalizing their relationship or believe that the church and state have no right to intervene in their personal lives (Barber and Axinn 1998; Elizabeth 1997, 2000; Rolfe and Peel 2011). Cohabitation is chosen by some because it is thought to involve less personal commitment, fewer obligations to their partner or his/her kin group, a less gendered division of labour, and the apparent option to leave without complications if the relationship is no longer mutually beneficial. However, when cohabiting relationships end in separation, the lack of legal protection sometimes leaves one partner with fewer assets and less income. This is especially relevant for different-sex couples who have children, where one partner (usually the man) has supported the family financially while the other (usually the woman) has provided unpaid domestic services and child care. Relationships that end under these circumstances often result in the impoverishment of mothers and children unless fathers continue to support them, mothers find well-paying jobs, and/or the state supplements their incomes.

Some policy-makers worry about the dramatic increase in births outside marriage because the lower stability rates of these relationships may have negative implications for children's well-being and increase the number of mothers with children relying on social welfare contributions. Relationships have certainly become less stable than in the past, and the rise in cohabitation has contributed to this (Beck-Gernsheim 2002). In addition, cohabiting fathers have a higher probability of separating from their partners than married fathers and subsequently a higher probability of losing contact with their children.

In summary, policy-makers have wondered whether the trend to non-marital cohabitation among different-sex individuals signals a fundamental change in attitudes about marriage, authority, and commitment to family. If cohabitation is just a new form of "courtship," this may seem less dangerous from the perspective of social conservatives, because it predicts that these couples will eventually marry as they mature (Baker 2010: 59). If cohabitation represents a more fundamental social change, it may signify a diminishing respect for the traditions of the church and state, and increased emphasis on personal choice, which could predict greater instability in future relationships. These societal changes would require a number of legal reforms, such as specifying the obligations of cohabiting partners to each other and to any children they may produce, and creating guidelines about the division of any property that separating couples might have accumulated during their cohabitation. The legal acceptance of widespread cohabitation could also open up debates about the decriminalization of other family forms such as polygamy (Beeby 2006), just as it has already opened up debates over the legal recognition of same-sex couples.

The Legalization of Same-Sex Relationships

More different-sex and same-sex couples now share a home without legal relationship recognition because they either believe that marriage offers little personal benefit or they oppose it as an exclusive, gendered, or heterosexist institution. At the same time, some gays and lesbians have fought assiduously for social recognition and legal rights (Einarsdottir 2011; Elizabeth 2001; McNair et al. 2002; Smart 2007b; Weeks 2007). The legalization of same-sex relationships has produced considerable debate about the changing nature of intimate relationships and the social meaning of marriage (Schecter et al. 2008; Shipman and Smart 2007; Smart 2008).

Denmark was the first country to enable same-sex couples to legalize their relationships in 1989 (Einarsdottir 2011). Since then, numerous jurisdictions (for example, Sweden, the Netherlands, Germany, France, Ireland, Spain, and Portugal) have changed their laws and regulations to legalize same-sex unions, while others (such as Australia) continue to debate the issue and its implications. In Canada, the federal Civil Marriages Act of July 2005 formally legalized same-sex marriage and by 2006, 17 percent of same-sex couples identified in the Canadian census were legally married (VIF 2007). Between 2006 and 2011 the number of same-sex couples marrying in Canada tripled, and married same-sex couples now make up 32.5 percent of all same-sex couples living together (Statistics Canada 2012).

A number of other jurisdictions initially created new legal categories called "civil union" (New Zealand, Hawaii, Illinois) or "civil partnership" (United Kingdom, Ireland), instead of opening marriage to same-sex couples (Rolfe and Peel 2011; UK Office of National Statistics 2010). In some jurisdictions, such as New Zealand, these new forms of legalization were also available to different-sex couples. In this country in 2009, 78 percent of civil unions were between same-sex couples, and 60 percent of these were between women (Statistics New Zealand 2011: 1). This is similar to the female majority in many Canadian provinces (Rothblum 2005) but varies from the male majority in the United Kingdom and parts of Northern Europe (Rolfe and Peele 2011; Waaldijik 2001). Although New Zealand legislated same-sex marriage in April 2013, at the time of our study, different-sex couples could choose between the two forms of legalization but 99.6 percent chose to marry (Statistics New Zealand 2012).

Civil unions/partnerships typically provide same-sex couples with some but not necessarily all of the recognitions and rights afforded married different-sex couples. However, the creation of civil unions/partnerships usually represents a political compromise between progressives and social conservatives that offers some rights and protection, while respecting the traditional idea that marriage is a partnership between a man and a woman for the purposes of child-bearing (Moore 2003). This compromise does not always placate calls for same-sex marriage, as evidenced in New Zealand where a bill was introduced to Parliament in 2012 to define marriage as a union of two people regardless of their sex, sexual orientation, or gender identity. This bill passed into law in April 2013.

The fight for same-sex marriage and civil unions/partnerships has been led mainly by social reformers who argue that human rights are violated when long-term same-sex relationships are not acknowledged or respected by the state or employers (Weeks 2007). Yet, legalizing same-sex unions has been strongly opposed by a number of religious groups, including the Catholic Church, fundamentalist Christians, and other social and political conservatives. Opponents tend to view civil unions/partnerships and same-sex relationships as threatening to Biblical teaching and to stable patterns of heterosexuality and reproduction, and both are seen as indicative of the decline of the traditional family, the institution of marriage, and public morality.

Civil unions/partnerships have been controversial among elements of gay and lesbian communities as well. Recent research finds that some same-sex couples choose not to legalize their relationships because they view civil union or partnership as a double-edged sword (Rolfe and Peel 2011). Creating a separate legal category, such as civil partnerships in the United Kingdom, has been perceived by some as a "consolation prize" for denying same-sex couples access to "real" marriage, and implies that their unions are inferior to those of heterosexuals.

Some gays and lesbians also feel that separate legislation (such as the civil partnerships legislation in the United Kingdom, which is only for same-sex couples) makes "hetero-normative" assumptions about the nature of their intimate relationships. In other words, it assumes that same-sex relationships are similar to "normal" heterosexual married relationships; but marriage has had a long history of gender inequalities sanctioned by the church and state. Some gays and lesbians see their relationships as more egalitarian and therefore different from marriage (Jowett and Peel 2010; Rolfe and Peel 2011; Smart 2011). Same-sex couples who legalize their relationships are required to mimic marriage in other ways too. They are expected to maintain a monogamous relationship, to share their income should one of them cease paid employment, and to share their property should they separate, even though they may not wish to do so.

Researchers have nevertheless found that same-sex cohabitants who choose to legalize their relationships tend to place a much greater emphasis than different-sex couples on the importance of social and legal recognition and a sense of familial belonging (Schecter et al. 2008; Shipman and Smart 2007; Sullivan 2004). The participants in these studies speak about wanting to make a public commitment to acknowledge their love and to celebrate their relationship, as well as to gain better links with kin, the respect and acknowledgement automatically granted to married heterosexual family members, and legal benefits and protection that have long been available to married heterosexual couples. Furthermore, the process of legalizing relationships for many same-sex couples is both personal and political because it contains an implicit critique of the marginalization of same-sex intimacy. Hence, it is not uncommon for same-sex weddings to entail a second "coming out," complete with all the attendant emotions that accompanied the first one (Baker and Elizabeth 2012c; Smart 2007b, 2008). However, the political nature of same-sex formalization prompts some couples to remain as cohabitants rather than legalizing their relationships.

The Rise of Independent Celebrants and the Wedding Industry

The increased use of independent celebrants, together with the global spread of the "wedding industry," has had a significant impact on expectations about weddings as well as actual wedding practices. When the state became involved in overseeing marriage over a hundred years ago, members of the clergy were licensed to marry couples, either in their churches or in other specified locations. The English-speaking jurisdictions also have a long history of civil wedding ceremonies in municipal registry offices, conducted by registry officials, judges, mayors, members of local council, and/ or justices of the peace. In the 1970s, Australia and New Zealand were the first English-speaking countries to expand the range of marriage celebrants and relax the rules about where and when weddings could take place. Since then, the profession of independent celebrant (or marriage "officiant" or "commissioner") has spread to other jurisdictions, including many states within the United States but not the United Kingdom. Some places, such as the Canadian province of Ontario, still require a minister, judge, justice of the peace, or clerk of the municipal court to conduct a legal wedding, and limit the type of place where these ceremonies can be conducted (Ontario Government 2012).

The introduction of celebrants who are independent of the state and the church has had several effects on wedding patterns. First, it has expanded the range of locations and timing of weddings, enabling a greater degree of personalization in ceremonies and their subsequent celebrations. Second, it has altered the gendered and sexual composition of those who preside over weddings. In the past, these were predominantly men who were either ministers of religion or justices of the peace. Now, many celebrants are women, who come to this position from a variety of occupational and social backgrounds. In New Zealand, for example, 61 percent of independent celebrants are female, although the majority of ministers of religion are still male (New Zealand Dept of Internal Affairs 2011). In addition, the legal recognition of same-sex couples has paved the way for openly gay, lesbian, or bisexual individuals to become independent celebrants.

The rise of independent celebrants is one of the factors accelerating the rise of personalized weddings that can be held in a variety of locations, including parks, historic properties, or commercialized wedding venues. However, a larger industry has also developed around these events, especially urging heterosexual brides to aspire to expensive and celebrity-like weddings. Predating World War II, the wedding industry has expanded in many countries since the 1970s, attempting to "commodify" much of the planning and preparation work previously done within families by brides and their mothers without remuneration (Blakely 2008). This industry includes wedding exhibitions and fashion shows, glossy magazines displaying outfits and celebration options, wedding planners who are paid to organize these events, secular celebrants who preside over but also help plan the ceremonies, and a rising number of commercial wedding venues such as historic houses, vineyards, and resorts. This industry, along with celebrity weddings and greater coverage of weddings in the media, helps to shape social expectations about the nature of "real weddings" and what they represent (Boden 2003; Ingraham 2008; Otnes and Pleck 2003).

Increasingly, resorts and other venues in "exotic" tourist destinations seek to attract couples who wish to solemnize and celebrate their union while on vacation. "Wedding tourism" contributes considerable funds to local economies and therefore is often promoted by governments as well as private entrepreneurs. Countries such as New Zealand have become destinations for overseas couples to legalize their relationships, especially for couples entering a civil union (Husbands 2006; Johnston 2006). About 10 percent of marriages and nearly 19 percent of civil unions in that country were registered to overseas residents in 2009, and many of these couples travelled from Australia and the United States (Statistics New Zealand 2010c). Clearly, weddings provide a significant source of revenue for many commercial businesses.

In our New Zealand study, outlined in the next section, we used marriage and civil union celebrants as well as long-term co-habitants to provide us with valuable information about wedding trends and practices.

Overview of Our Empirical Research

The ideas outlined in this book are derived from a comprehensive overview of previous research on cohabitation and marriage, focusing on findings from Canada and the English-speaking countries. In addition, we present the results of our qualitative interviews from New Zealand, drawing on the verbatim comments from our participants in order to supplement and expand on the findings of previous research. The voices or personal stories of our participants highlight their understandings of cohabitation and what it means to marry or have a civil union, and illustrates their interpersonal negotiations and the social influences involved in the transition from cohabitation to marriage. In the Methodological Appendix at the end of this book, we provide further details of our research design and methodology, but we also present an abbreviated version in this section. We begin with a brief overview of the conceptual framework behind our research.

Conceptual Framework

Conceptually, the book focuses on intimate relationships within the wider social context, and is situated mainly within interpretive and symbolic interaction theories. These theories typically argue that the meanings associated with particular actions or behaviours are "socially constructed" and shaped by who we are in terms of characteristics such as our sex, age, sexual orientation, social class and cultural background, and socio-economic status. Our beliefs and behaviours are also influenced by the ways that we present ourselves to others and especially by the ways that other people interpret, ignore, resist, or reinforce our actions and shape our identity (Goffman 1959; Tombaugh 2009).

In this book, we also emphasize that the transition from non-residential dating to cohabitation and from cohabitation to marriage or civil union, is not simply a *couple* decision but often requires considerable negotiation between partners, who may have different personal goals, values, and expectations of the relationship. Furthermore, whether or not to marry and the timing of marriage are also influenced by the ideas and practices of their friends and family members, especially their parents and siblings (Manning et al. 2011; Scanzoni 1982; Smart 2007b).

In considering the social context, we acknowledge that women and men, as well as different-sex and same-sex couples, sometimes make different "choices" based on their family circumstances, upbringing, and subsequent life experiences. Despite changes in the status of women, men and women continue to have differential access to interpersonal power and material resources, which shapes their priorities and choices. For example, men typically earn more money than women, and more often expect to become family earners with uninterrupted lifetime careers (Baker 2010). Not surprisingly, the timing of marriage has historically been more strongly connected to the man's earning capacity than the woman's, as women tend to earn less but also expect to take employment leave or reduce their working hours for child-bearing and child-raising.

In the twenty-first century, men are still expected to propose to women, but when a heterosexual woman initiates a marriage proposal, researchers have found that the engagement is seldom announced until the proposal is repeated by the man (Sassler and Miller 2011). In addition, women are expected to spend more time on and extract more pleasure from making wedding arrangements (Blakely 2008; Boden 2001). Studies have also found that heterosexual men are more likely than heterosexual women to report lower levels of commitment in romantic relationships and to control relationship transitions (such as from cohabitation to marriage) as well as wedding budgets (Sassler and Miller 2011; Stanley et al. 2006). These gendered patterns form the backdrop to our qualitative study and form a key part of our overall research, including the interpretation of our interview material.

Our conceptual framework also highlights the role of advertising and representations from the media in shaping consumer desires and spending patterns, which may also vary by gender and sexual orientation (Boden 2003; Ingraham 2008). We discuss the ways that the "wedding industry" encourages couples to aspire to expensive engagement and wedding rings, wedding outfits, venues, and honeymoon trips that often cost more than couples and their families can afford. Popular culture typically portrays "the wedding" as the ultimate event in a girl's life or as an opportunity to become a celebrity for the day, which encourages consumer-oriented behaviour. Back in the nineteenth century, the American sociologist Thorstein Veblen (1899) developed the concept of "conspicuous consumption" to refer to the public use of clothing, jewellery, and expensive entertaining to reveal or flaunt one's social status. We also adopt this concept in our discussion of the portrayal of wedding practices but also refer to Andrew Cherlin's work (2010) on weddings as markers of prestige.

The Interviews

With these conceptual ideas in mind, in 2011 we completed qualitative interviews with fifty participants living in New Zealand, including ten marriage/civil union celebrants and forty individuals who had been cohabiting for at least three years and either intended to legalize their relationship or had already done so. We chose to interview celebrants because we saw them as key informants on marriage practices. Long-term cohabitants were interviewed because previous research has shown that this group is less likely to expect to marry and thus less likely to view cohabitation as part of an explicit pathway to marriage than those cohabiting for shorter periods (Coast 2009; Manning and Smock 2002; Qu 2003). This finding raises interesting questions about what prompts long-term cohabitants to formalize their unions.

We interviewed all of the participants in their homes in Auckland (New Zealand's largest city) for about one hour each, digitally recording the interviews and later transcribing them in full. New Zealand provided a good venue for this research because the government treats both different-sex and same-sex cohabitants as "married" when they have lived together for three years, and if they later separate requires them to divide their assets equally in the same manner as married couples. The government has also created two kinds of legal union: marriage (for different-sex couples) and civil union (for both same-sex and different-sex couples).

The New Zealand government already considers long-term cohabitants, both different-sex and same-sex, to be in a "marriage-like relationship" for the purposes of spousal support, taxation, and social benefits. After sharing a residence for three years, separating couples in New Zealand are required by law to equally divide any property accrued during their cohabitation or marriage. Biological and adoptive parents, regardless of their marital status, are required to financially support their children. But same-sex partners cannot become adoptive parents, and may be more at risk than cohabiting different-sex couples of being denied recognition as next of kin, even though New Zealand law extended status recognition to all cohabiting couples irrespective of their sexual orientation in 2005 (Inglis 2007). Thus, the legal differences between cohabiting couples and those who are married or in a civil union are much less significant than they once were, partly because many governments and social agencies now provide legal and institutional benefits for couples irrespective of marital status (Heuveline and Timberlake 2004).

In our interviews, the celebrant sample was "purposive" (searching for specific categories of people) and selected from several celebrant and church websites. We wanted to interview older celebrants who had been marrying couples for many years, as well as younger ones who were more recently registered by the government. We deliberately sought out males and females, different-sex and same-sex celebrants, those who were registered to perform marriages and/or civil unions, and secular celebrants and ministers of religion. Although this part of the sample seems small, these celebrants had collectively already performed over fifteen hundred marriages and hundreds of civil union ceremonies.

The gender and age distribution of the celebrant sample reflected many of the characteristics of celebrants in Auckland, with seven women and three men who ranged in age from twenty-eight to sixty-three, with most over forty-five. They typically had university degrees in the social sciences or theology and four were ministers of religion, although two of these were also registered as independent celebrants. (Additional details are found in the Methodological Appendix at the end of this book.) In addition to questions about personal circumstances and training, we asked them about the patterns and trends they saw in wedding ceremonies and subsequent celebrations, why they thought that many long-term cohabiting couples proceeded to formalize their relationships, and the advantages and disadvantages of doing so. The exact interview questions we used can be found in the Appendix. In the analysis, we mapped each celebrant's answers, searched for patterns or similar answers, and extracted illustrative verbatim comments on key themes.

The second stage of the project involved forty interviews with individuals who had been cohabiting for at least three years and had already legalized their unions or were planning to do so in the near future. This volunteer sample was obtained from formal and informal advertisements but it was also purposive, because we sought to include certain categories of people. We wanted to include a wide age range of men and women, including those planning to marry or enter a civil union, and those who had already formalized their unions. We also set out to over-represent civil unions due to the small amount of research on this form of legalization. Among those who had entered civil unions, we wanted to include gays, lesbians, and heterosexuals.

Additional details of the cohabitation sample can be found in the Methodological Appendix but this sample ranged in age from twenty-eight to sixty-two. At the time of the interview, most participants were already married or in a civil union, while the rest were "engaged" or about to formalize their relationship. The volunteer nature of the sample led to an over-representation of women and university-educated participants, although the sample was nevertheless diverse in terms of birthplace, age, education, occupation, sexual orientation, social class, and cultural background. Our interview questions focused on how and why participants came to be cohabiting, how they eventually decided to legalize their relationship, and details of their planned or actual wedding. We also asked how their decision to formalize their relationship were interpreted by friends and family, and whether they anticipated or perceived any change afterward. The full interview schedule for the cohabitants is also included in the Methodological Appendix.

In the analysis of the interviews, we searched for common themes in their verbatim comments, and compared the comments made by the celebrants and cohabitants, the men and the women, both members of a couple, those entering marriage and civil union, older and younger participants, and same-sex and different-sex couples. Qualitative interviews cannot be used to generalize all cohabitants who are legalizing their relationships, as the sample is not representative even of the population of New Zealand. Instead, the rich and subjective verbatim comments from celebrants and cohabitants are used to enhance our understanding of findings from the wider research, and to provide further insights and illustrations about relationships, living arrangements, and weddings in the twenty-first century.

The main contribution of this book is to provide a broad overview of research findings about the transition from cohabitation to marriage in the English-speaking countries, but also to offer a higher level of personal and social detail derived from our interviews in New Zealand. This level of detail relates particularly to interpersonal negotiations, gendered aspirations, unique marriage proposals, and numerous examples of wedding practices, details which cannot be ascertained from quantitative studies that focus mainly on statistical correlations among variables. The voices of our participants and their social circumstances, as well as our interpretations of their meaning and significance, serve to deepen our understanding of the transition from cohabitation to marriage in an individualistic and consumer-oriented society. Our interviews reveal the range of values, beliefs, and practices, but also highlight some of the enduring gendered patterns in intimate relationships.

We combine our interview material with previous research from several other countries to help explain why cohabiting couples decide to legalize their relationships when there is increasing acceptance of cohabitation, especially among different-sex couples. Furthermore, both different-sex and same-sex cohabitants enjoy many (although not all) of the legal rights, protections, and responsibilities accorded to married couples. We also want to know how our participants negotiate the transition from cohabitation to marriage, and how they solemnize and celebrate this significant rite of passage/ritual. These findings can then be compared to those from other jurisdictions.

Conclusions: Is Marriage Still a Cultural Ideal?

In all the English-speaking countries, marriage rates have declined as cohabitation rates have increased, but previous research shows that most cohabitants who stay together eventually formalize their relationships (Baker 2010; Baxter, Haines, and Hewitt 2010). Our book investigates the transition from cohabitation to marriage, and the meanings attributed to marriage (or civil union/civil partnership) compared to cohabitation. We are particularly interested in the symbolic nature of marriage as a cultural ideal or marker of distinction and prestige. The wider research indicates that after years of cohabitation and even child-bearing, same-sex and different-sex couples typically want to celebrate their commitment to each other publicly, but in a unique and personal way. Nevertheless, decisions to marry and wedding practices continue to be influenced by legal requirements; social pressures from family, friends, and the lucrative "wedding industry"; and from cultural ideas about love, romance, and marriage.

The arguments in this book are based on our own interviews in New Zealand and numerous studies mainly from the other English-speaking countries. This combined research suggests that cohabiting couples do not always initially agree about if and when to marry but often negotiate with each other about the advantages/disadvantages, the timing, and the format of their wedding. The decision to marry is sometimes made after extenuating circumstances, such as an unexpected pregnancy, a divorce, or a family dispute relating to their partner. In addition, many marriage decisions and ceremonies continue to be stage-managed symbolic events, which make public the couple's already private commitment, but also highlight gender differences. Weddings also provide opportunities to celebrate "successful" relationships with family and friends.

The research also suggests that couples increasingly expect their weddings to be memorable life events that draw on elements of tradition while reflecting the couple's beliefs and lifestyle. Weddings also announce who participants are in terms of gender, social class, and sexual orientation. For some couples, modern weddings provide another avenue for "conspicuous consumption" in a consumer-oriented society, while for others weddings are largely do-it-yourself occasions that follow in the footsteps of do-it-yourself biographies of love. The social and commercial influences on wedding patterns and practices are also discussed in this book.

In the next chapter, we focus on the decision-making or negotiating processes that couples experience when they make the transition from dating to cohabitation and from cohabitation to marriage or civil union/partnership.

CHAPTER 2

Negotiating Transitions: From Dating to Cohabitation to "Marriage"

Introduction

This chapter investigates the circumstances surrounding an initial cohabitation, and why and how cohabitants decide whether or not to formalize their relationships. Our discussion includes an examination of the timing of the legalization decision and how this decision is negotiated between partners. We consider variations brought about by factors such as age, previous marital experience, and sexual preference, but also investigate whether decisions to legalize relationships are the outcome of formal "proposals" or arise from conversations about their mutual desire to spend their lives together or the pros and cons of marriage or civil union. We also explore the role of social pressure in the making of this decision, including the implicit and explicit expectations of parents, the couple's children (if there are any), other relatives, friends, and other associates. In particular, we are interested in interpersonal reasons as well as events that might encourage partners to formalize their relationship or make a public commitment. Such events could include a health emergency, an unexpected pregnancy, the granting of a divorce from a previous marriage, concerns expressed by children or parents, or lack of respect or acknowledgement of a same-sex relationship.

First, we examine the research findings, including from our interviews, about how couples initially come to live together, sometimes with no intention of marrying. Second, we discuss why so many cohabiting couples later decide to formalize their relationship even when one or both partners were previously indifferent or opposed to marriage or civil union. In both cases, we provide verbatim comments from our own interviews with celebrants and cohabitants.

Progressing Couple Relationships from Dating to Cohabitation

Most couples in Canada and the English-speaking countries live together before marriage or civil union/partnership, especially those who are younger, not particularly religious, have lower incomes, and/or are in same-sex partnerships (Baker 2010). In the past, different-sex couples would have "dated" while continuing to live with their parents. After reaching a point of commitment, they would have become formally "engaged," a period of time that would have last for months or years, and then married before sharing a home. The engagement period not only enabled others to start viewing the couple as lifetime partners but it also enabled the couple to save money for their wedding and future home, and to spend more private time together. Now, sexual intercourse outside marriage has become more socially acceptable between heterosexual couples, unplanned pregnancies are easier to prevent, and same-sex relationships have acquired greater legitimacy. These social changes make it easier for couples to live together earlier in their relationship. While some couples engage in "co-residential dating," research indicates that for many couples cohabitation is pursued as part of a process of relationship progression, even though marriage as the endpoint of this progression is seldom explicitly discussed when couples first move in together (Lindsay 2000). In other words, for many couples cohabitation functions as a "trial marriage," although this may only become apparent in hindsight.

Non-religious couples, in particular, typically view cohabitation as a practical solution to a number of logistical problems: how to pay for two homes when living expenses are high, where to live when one partner cannot find suitable accommodation, and how to find more time to spend together when both are employed. As both Australian and American researchers have documented, cohabiting couples often "slide" from dating into cohabitation with little active decision-making about the long-term future of their relationship. These couples typically viewed cohabitation as something that "just happened" because it was "convenient" and not something that symbolized a "significant commitment" (Lindsay 2000; Stanley et al. 2006). Lindsay (2000) claims that cohabitation is the outcome of an ambiguous transition that generates an ambiguous commitment and status. According to Stanley et al. (2006), the ambiguity is a product of the increase in the level of "constraint commitment," brought about by barriers or constraints to separation once a couple moves in together and shares their possessions, without any necessary corresponding increase in their level of feeling for or dedication to each other.

Researchers have found that relationship progressions from casual encounters to dating, from dating to cohabitation, and from cohabitation to marriage among different-sex couples are more likely to be controlled by men than women (Bogle 2008; Sassler and Miller 2011). In addition, relational progression occurs in a context where couples typically believe that they need to accomplish a set of goals before they marry, which often relate to earning capacity, savings, and home ownership (Cherlin 2004; Hewitt and Baxter 2012). However, these goals appear to be harder for couples to attain now than in previous decades.

Compared to the 1970s, both male and female workers now need higher formal qualifications to secure full-time jobs, especially professional or managerial positions. Most households also feel that they need two incomes to survive because housing and general living costs have increased relative to income, and young people have raised their aspirations about living standards. In different-sex couples, both men and women usually expect the man rather than the woman to be able to support an anticipated family before transitioning to marriage (Carmichael and Whittaker 2007a; Duvander 1999; Qu 2003). Thus, despite considerable changes in gender relations over the last fifty years, the marriage-worthiness of heterosexual men continues to be based on highly gendered assumptions about the division of labour that should take place within marriage, especially after the birth of children.

Many couples begin to cohabit without any concrete intention of marrying. They simply want to enjoy the here and now of their relationship and are curious about how it will develop over time. This may be especially the case for same-sex couples for whom legalization has not been a possibility until recently, which means they are less likely to see marriage as part of their future trajectory. However, even a couple who become more committed to each other and say that they want to spend their lives together tend to postpone their wedding until they can see some concrete reason to formalize their relationship and until they are certain that they have made the right choice of partner. As separation and divorce rates among different-sex couples have soared since the 1970s (Cherlin 2010), the social embarrassment, cost, and inconvenience of getting a divorce seems to outweigh some of the negative social reactions to living together outside marriage (Edin and Kefalas 2005). While many different-sex cohabitants separate before making a long-term commitment, those who stay together typically decide to marry after three to five years of cohabitation, although some take much longer.

In our study, the celebrants confirmed the findings of official statistics and other research by noting that all or the vast majority of the couples they married were already living together before the wedding, including a few couples who cohabited for more than ten years. Some had already bought houses and had children together, while many weddings involved remarriages for at least one member of the couple. The celebrants commented on the pattern of widespread premarital cohabitation among different-sex couples and noted how rapidly it has become socially acceptable, except among particularly religious people. As one female independent celebrant (who had also been a minister of religion) said:

I think there's been a whole cultural shift with couples. I think it's become far more acceptable that couples live together. I think that's still *not* the case in a church community . . . within the Christian community there is still very much an expectation that if you choose the person that you're going to live with for the rest of your life, you choose to get married. You don't try it out first. But within the wider community I think it's much more acceptable to live together.

This same celebrant, now in her fifties, talked about modern cohabitation for different-sex couples as a new stage between dating and marriage that continues until the couple makes a firmer commitment to remain together. She also suggested that once couples begin cohabiting, the reasons for marriage sometimes diminish for a few years but usually resurface later when they want to "settle down," buy a house, and reproduce:

In my parent's generation . . . there wasn't that sort of *in between*, but now . . . the couple decides that they're . . . not just dating, you know they are serious about each other, so the next step is that they tend to move in together and I think often couples tend to think: "well why the big deal of marriage? Do we want to go through all that hassle, the expense?" They're often planning to travel. There's a lot of young couples that I've dealt with that . . . once they've done their training and then they've started their jobs and then got into their profession, they then have a bit of time to travel and maybe even work overseas, and so the thought of actually planning a wedding kind of doesn't fit that time in their lives. Whereas once they start thinking of coming back home, maybe starting a family, buying a house together. . . . I think that's often the trigger that they actually realize that even though they've been living in the "now," and feel that the other person is right for them "now," I think they do start looking more long term and thinking well actually this is the person that I want to be with in the future as well.

We explicitly asked the cohabiting participants how they came to be living together. Many provided romantic reasons, such as being in love and wanting to share a future together, but they also spoke of practical reasons, such as lack of accommodation for one partner, the need to share housing costs, and the desire to spend more time together. For example, a recently married woman said:

I wasn't really going to be able to afford to live by myself or find a flat (apartment) that would take a [large dog] in so I ended up living with [male partner]. It wasn't like something I didn't want to do. It kind of made sense at the time in terms of our relationship as well but it was quite affected by those factors.

Another married woman made a similar comment:

We'd both been living in a flatting situation, not that far from one another and we'd sort of spent time at each other's flats, and then my now husband looked at buying a house. He was sort of looking for a house, I think, when we met and he bought a house . . . and I moved in soon after that with him and we just kind of worked on the house, there was a lot to do and I guess [the cohabitation] probably came about because we were spending so much time at each other's places anyway and I think we felt that we had certainty of our future together. So we decided that it would be best that we both lived in the same place and pooled not just financial resources but our kind of weekends and time to actually work on the house. It needed quite a bit of work. . . . I think he made the offer of me moving there and it just seemed to be a sensible move for me.

Among our different-sex participants, women typically moved into the man's home rather than the other way around, partly because he was likely to be older with a higher income and more assets, but also because he was more likely to take the initiative and invite her to cohabit with him. However, not all participants shared this pattern, especially women who came from divorced parents or held feminist values. For example, a forty-year-old female participant who got married several years ago told the interviewer:

> My mum has been married three times and I've seen her go through two bad divorces, and women get really hurt, everything gets taken from them. I'm very much a believer, you've got to protect yourself, especially financially . . . . I sold my house and bought the house in [suburb of Auckland] for [partner] and I to live in. So that was the first time we had our own home, but I owned it, it was mine and he paid rent. And I paid all the rates and everything. . . . I didn't want to share an asset, I needed to be in control and [to] control what's happening.

Both same-sex and different-sex couples talked of the advantages of cohabitation over living in separate homes. For example, a lesbian woman now in a civil union explained her reasons for cohabiting: "Yeah just convenience with some stuff and being able to spend more time together, and having your life a little bit more organized." A gay man about forty years old in a same-sex civil union made similar comments about the advantages of cohabitation:

> Well there are loads [of advantages]. Trying to go from one place to another just logistically it's a nightmare. It's cost beneficial to live together but also I mean at the end of the day it just means you get to spend more time together when you're both working. You only get a few hours left in the day either side that you can see each other. So if you are compatible, there's no real reason why you should live separately.

In a confirmation of the findings of other research (Lindsay 2000), many of the participants in our study reported no marriage plans when they initially cohabited. One gay man put it starkly when he said: "I mean people don't start living together and start talking about marriage straight away." And another 30-year-old married heterosexual woman talked about their early years of co-habitation in the following manner:

> I don't think [marriage] was a priority for either of us. There were other things we wanted to do, like travel, buy a house. I don't think either of us saw the need to formalize the relationship at that point. We were always sort of quite comfortable with our commitment to each other. I think we were both on the same page from quite an early point in the relationship . . . . And [partner] especially is sort of very non-religious and at first I think saw [marriage] mainly as a religious institution and sort of not really kind of relevant, I guess.

Clearly, widespread changes are apparent in relationship formation and reformation, as well as the order of relationship events, and both celebrants and cohabitants commented on these new patterns in our interviews. A recently married female participant around thirty years old epitomized these social changes when she said: "We thought if we keep waiting until we can afford a house, or until we can afford that or this or whatever, we'll never have kids. So we kind of did it backwards and we had kids first and then we got a house and a mortgage and all that stuff [and then got married]." This pattern is becoming increasingly prevalent in all of the English-speaking countries. In the next section, we address the various motivations for cohabitants to marry.

Motives to Formalize Relationships

Despite the prevalence of cohabitation and growing beliefs among many cohabitants that marriage is no longer necessary, a number of researchers have found that marriage continues to be viewed in the larger society as a highly symbolic act (Cherlin 2004; Gross 2005; Qu et al. 2009). As more couples cohabit early in their relationship, an important reason to formalize the union is making a shift from a private to a public commitment, thereby creating an excuse to celebrate their "successful" and enduring relationship and ensure that it is properly acknowledged by family and friends. Couples, both different- and same-sex, also marry to create a more secure environment for the rearing of children; to develop a solid social, economic, or legal basis for the relationship; to accommodate the social pressure from family and friends in the case of different-sex couples or, in relation to some same-sex couples, to gain greater acceptance and recognition from family members (Carmichael and Whittaker 2007b; Duvander 1999; Jamieson et al. 2002; Lewis 2001; Shipman and Smart 2007; Smock et al. 2005; Steele et al. 2005). We examine each of these reasons separately. These motives to marry are not mutually exclusive and many of our participants gave multiple reasons for their decision to marry.

Shifting to Public Commitment and Celebrating Successful Relationships

In the wider research as well as our interviews, the most prevalent reason given for formalizing an intimate relationship is to make a public commitment, enabling the couple's already private commitment to be acknowledged and their love for each other to be celebrated by friends and family. Participants in our study spoke about their desire for a public commitment in terms of gaining acknowledgement from others of the permanent nature of their intimate relationship or publicly celebrating the fact that their relationship has already endured years of hard times as well as good times. Others in our study offered a more casual explanation by claiming it was an "excuse for a good party" with family and friends.

The celebrants in our study normally asked their clients in the initial meeting why they planned to marry, in order to gain some understanding of their personal circumstances and wedding preferences and expectations. Most of these celebrants reported that long-term cohabitants implied that they were moving to a *higher* level of commitment when they made the decision to marry. Some added that after marriage, clients say that others view their relationship differently, especially senior family members. For example, a female celebrant, who only presided over same-sex civil unions, aptly commented that with a wedding:

You're saying, this is *not* just my, you know, my "bonk du jour." This is *not* just the person I happen to be living with now, we'll probably break up in a while and I'll move on. You're saying, this is the person I choose to be with for as long as I choose that, and I intend for that to be a forever sort of thing. And I know that there are some couples who I've spoken to subsequently who've said their families have treated them differently afterwards.

The desire to make a public commitment and to celebrate a relationship is a motive for both different-sex and same-sex couples to legalize their relationships. For example, a female celebrant in our study commented:

Whether it's marriage or civil union, it's a chance for both sides of their families, their friends, their history, you know their supporters, their loved ones, it's a chance for them all to come together and to celebrate and to have this focus as this couple and . . . even though they might have been living together for years . . . it's the whole celebration thing and actually stating in public how they feel about each other.

When discussing the similarities and differences between marriage and civil unions, most of the celebrants focused on straight/queer similarities, because most civil unions in New Zealand involve same-sex couples. A female celebrant spoke about same-sex civil unions when she said: "You know it's basically two people who have come to love each other, who have lived together, who have decided . . . to spend their future together, which is exactly the same as a couple moving towards marriage. It's the same commitment thing."

Most of the cohabitants in our study also focused on the public commitment motive, suggesting that they loved each other and had already made a private commitment to each other, but now wanted to make this commitment more public and celebratory. A young married woman suggested that marriage actually represented a higher level of commitment than cohabitation for them when she said:

> I think that for us personally, marriage signified a commitment to each other that hadn't existed when we were just living together, but that's not to say that people who just live together couldn't have that same commitment. It's nice to have a celebration of that in front of all your friends and family.

Similarly, a young gay male in a civil union explained his reasons for formalizing his relationship: "It was just about celebrating our love. . . . It's irrelevant that we are both men . . . what is relevant is that our love is pure and our love is real. . . . So I didn't want it to be taken for granted, I wanted to ensure that we shared that with everyone . . . " The importance of public acknowledgement was also made explicit by an older woman, who had been cohabiting with her lesbian partner for over twenty years, when she said: "Before the Civil Union Act came into being, I had wanted a commitment ceremony because there wasn't anything else available for same-sex relationships, legally. But it was more that I wanted our relationship to be acknowledged and celebrated."

Some cohabitants expressed the desire for a public celebration within the context of negotiating difficult relationships over a long-term cohabitation. For example, this young woman who had shared a home with her male partner for seven years and had recently entered a different-sex civil union said:

> The main motivation [for our civil union] was to be able to have some kind of acknowledgement for our friends and family of how much we have appreciated their support through the ups and downs of the preceding seven years. . . . And just kind of a public declaration of this is permanent.

A married mother in her forties expressed a similar idea:

I guess I quite liked the idea of acknowledging our relationship with all our friends and celebrating that because we'd been together a long time. We'd gone through a lot of stuff. We'd had a baby and it just seemed like a nice time to . . . just celebrate that with all the people that we really cared about.

In our interviews, both same-sex and different-sex couples entering marriage or civil union focused on making a public commitment as the primary reason for formalizing their relationship. However, not all long-term cohabitants could clearly articulate their reasons for wanting to marry or have a civil union, and some made comments such as: "Why not?" Still others said: "It seems like the next stage," implying that they were progressing to a different stage in their relationship.

In some cases, even the marriage celebrants found the decision to formalize difficult to understand, although they assumed the couples were moving to a higher level of commitment and—as marriage celebrants—naturally approved of their decision. As one celebrant said:

I've got a couple that I'm marrying . . . and they've been together twenty-three years. They got together when he had two boys and she had three girls and . . . and now they've got grandchildren and now they've decided to get married and they've actually been engaged for eight years. . . . So when they came and sat here, I just thought once again: "there's no reason for them to get married. . . . They just seemed happy together after twenty-three years . . . " So I don't know what the answer is there. I think it's still really lovely. It's still maybe just another step in their commitment to each other.

The move to a different stage in their relationship may reflect the couple's desire to share a future together or what Stanley and colleagues (2006) call "dedication commitment." However, it may also be the result of a sense of the inevitability of being together into the future, something that they call "relationships inertia." Relationship inertia is a relatively common feature of cohabiting relationships because cohabitation, compared to dating, is characterized by an increase in the barriers or constraints to ending a relationship, without necessarily producing a rise in a couple's dedication to each other (ibid). Interestingly, the experience of relationship inertia may well be gendered. Compared to women, men may be less likely to marry because they are dedicated to the future of their relationship but more likely to marry as a result of relationship inertia (Rhoades, Stanley, and Markman 2009). A number of our participants told stories which suggested that women were more interested in marrying, presumably as a sign of the couple's dedication to each other. For instance, when we asked our participants whose idea it was to get married, one of the men, whose parents had divorced, said:

> Hers for sure. I tried my hardest to avoid it. Even once we got engaged I think I had the engagement ring thrown at me about three or four times because I was always saying that I find getting married stupid. . . . I almost got married against my will. It was awesome. I mean I'm so happy. It became like a war of attrition, so I suppose she gets that win.

Providing a Suitable Environment for Child-Rearing

The desire to have children remains a significant motivator for converting cohabiting relationships into publicly recognized ones, and researchers have found that couples who are not intending to bear children are less likely to legally marry (Qu et al. 2009). Even in the twenty-first century, different-sex marriage is widely seen as the basis of the "right" home environment for children and for their recognition by relatives as "legitimate" (Berrington 2001; Jamieson et al. 2002; Kirby 2008; Steele et al. 2005). Although governments and social agencies have abolished most of the distinctions between legitimate and illegitimate children, different-sex married couples particularly expect to gain approval and support from their family and friends during their child-bearing years.

Despite these sentiments, the number of ex-nuptial births has continued to rise across the West. In Canada, about 40 percent of children were born outside marriage in 2009 (VIF 2012), while 16.3 percent of children lived with cohabiting parents in 2011 (Statistics Canada 2012). In New Zealand, nearly 50 percent of births are ex-nuptial, although most of these are born to cohabiting parents. However, the fact that only 13 percent of children are living with cohabiting adults at any one time suggests that most couples marry before or shortly after they have children, and that most divorced parents with young children remarry (Pryor and Roberts 2005). Also in New Zealand, 8 percent of men and 26 percent of women who reported to be living in same-sex partnerships had a least one child living with them in 2006 (Statistics New Zealand 2010a: 12). In Canada, about 9 percent of same-sex couples had children living with them, and lesbian couples were much more likely than gay couples to be in this situation at 16.3 percent compared to 2.9 percent in 2006 (Statistics Canada 2007a). A similar percentage of gay and lesbian couples have children living with them in Australia (de Vaus 2004).

In our study, the celebrants reported that couples planning to become parents or who were already parents often married with the intention of creating a more secure social and legal environment for their children. For example, an older gay celebrant who officiated at both marriage and civil-union ceremonies said:

> People aren't getting married then living together. They're living together and then getting married, and they usually get married at the stage where they're thinking about starting a family. I think there's a feeling that marriage makes the relationship more stable. I don't think it does but that's the perception.

A female celebrant also suggested that both same-sex and different-sex couples tend to legalize their relationships when they have children: "One [lesbian] couple I can think of had a baby . . .

and now they were getting more 'unioned'. So it's kind of no different than all their straight friends."

The cohabitants in our study also talked about pregnancy and
children as motives for legalizing their relationship. For example, a
mother around forty years old, who married in her mid-twenties,
commented:

> For us the big thing was deciding to have children. And that was
> sort of moving our relationship to a different level too. I mean we
> were committed before that, but it was about something else, it
> was about there was going to be more people, we were going to
> have a family. So as part of that discussion about how we were go-
> ing to raise this child, [partner] said that he very strongly wanted
> to get married.

Some of the same-sex couples in our study also linked their
decision to formalize their relationship with their plans to have
children together. For instance, a young woman in a same-sex relationship, who was involved in a pregnancy insemination on their
wedding day, explicitly linked their wedding to a desire to have children and form a family when she said:

> For me it's around having, because we're trying to have children,
> and it's around . . . conforming to an idea of the heterosexual fam-
> ily. Which again really doesn't sit easily with me, but I know at the
> same time I've got to do it to make things easier for children . . . .
> Which is why I've also changed my name since the civil union . . .
> so that we would be seen as a family unit and you know, like yeah,
> very much subscribing to this heterosexual notion of what a fam-
> ily is, even though we don't really want to do that but we kind of
> have to make it okay for our children.

Another young woman who was planning a civil union with
her same-sex partner also associated getting married with starting
a family:

We like the idea of having the union first and then having a family. (Interviewer: *Why is that?*) For me I think it's about creating a really solid base and there's a sense of commitment for a long term, for a life together. . . . I mean neither of us are religious but that idea of marriage and then babies kind of just seems really Christian, it seems to make sense and fit for me.

Sometimes the decision by different-sex couples to marry during pregnancy was made in conjunction with expressions of social disapproval of their unmarried status made by older relatives. For example, another woman in her mid-forties, who has been married for ten years, recalls their "decision" to marry:

I was just heavily pregnant with [child's name]. I do remember my mother-in-law saying that [partner's] great aunt felt it was really bad that we weren't married. I mean she is obviously from a generation which is . . . I mean our parents didn't really care. I think they were just quite glad there was a grandchild on the way. . . . And I guess it just came from there really. I mean I guess for me it's probably always percolated around but I've never really said much about it. Maybe at that point with having a baby I sort of thought, well why not marry? When I brought the subject up, [partner] was just, "oh well, if you want to do that, that's fine."

Yet another woman in her forties, who married several years ago, talked about the importance of their child in stabilizing their relationship and encouraging them to marry:

Certainly when we had the baby, things got a lot more solid. . . . I guess we were just in a really good place and we'd bought a house and had a baby and everything just seemed good and settled and we were happy and it just seemed like a good time to celebrate all that, yeah. But I would say that it would have been a long, long time before we got to feeling that way.

Other participants offered additional pragmatic reasons to marry that were occasionally mixed with ambivalence. Decisions to marry in the context of ambivalence may indicate the presence of "relationship inertia," where couples "slide" into marriage after a period of cohabitation because the barriers to separation have incrementally increased to the point where going separate ways has become difficult. Alternatively, ambivalence might arise out of an initial rejection of marriage on philosophical grounds.

Pragmatic and Legal Reasons to Marry

Some of our study participants who were initially opposed to the idea of marriage reluctantly went through with the ceremony for pragmatic reasons. For example, a woman in her sixties talked about marrying for immigration reasons:

> We lived together for nineteen years and then I got my scholarship to go and do my PhD in [foreign country] and I needed to marry [partner] to take him. So there was just simply a practical reason for us getting married . . . . I have tended to feel that marriage is sort of for people who are insecure about things, that it's about ownership and possession . . . in fact it was sort of a bit of a cop out. . . . So we did sort of have a few talks about, "oh, are we really going to do this?" . . . Then a friend who was already over there said: "look, just go and get married. There's going to be other things that will be difficult. Just go and do it and get it out of the way."

Other participants reported that they married for emotional reasons but also because they believed there were pragmatic gains to be had from marriage. For example, a young man about to enter a different-sex civil union said:

> We were starting to think about getting a house, and that's a lot easier if you're married from the bank's point of view and everything like that. It just came to a point where we figured heck, we may as well do it. I'm probably not as romantic about all these sort

of things as I should be. But it definitely seemed like, yeah, it was a really good relationship. I kind of knew that I wanted to spend the rest of my life with her, all those mushy things. So it just sort of, yeah, it seemed like the natural thing to do.

In our study, both different-sex and same-sex participants mentioned the acquisition of legal rights when they talked about their motives to formalize their relationships but same-sex individuals were more likely to focus on the equity aspects. This suggests that motivational factors for legalizing relationships are often similar for straight and gay/lesbian couples, although more same-sex participants emphasized their vulnerability in the absence of social protections or legal rights. Particularly, older same-sex participants spoke of the importance of legalization in preventing and responding to family disputes, especially in relation to the division of assets or complex health-related decisions. For example, this gay man in his fifties and in a twenty-year relationship said:

> If you're gay there's a long history of quite negative things possibly happening around death, siblings and parents taking over because there are no legal rights in the bad old days up until quite recently. I know people this has happened to, long-standing partners have just been shunted out of the picture and the legal relatives have taken over. . . . We'd had some legal arrangements around assets in place before that but going for the civil union sort of rationalized it in a way that wasn't possible before.

He went on to say: "The civil union was part of that process of legal documentation and protection and just making sure everything was in place, protecting each other I suppose." His male partner made a similar comment when he talked about a family funeral where relatives disputed the will: "It was within that week that [the idea of having a civil union] had obviously been preying on both our minds and it just came up at that point. Nothing romantic about it at all! It was purely a legal thing."

Another participant, a lesbian woman in her fifties, told a story about the transformation of her stance toward to civil unions, going from vocal opposition to ambivalent acceptance following a thirty-five–minute venomous "barrage of hate about lesbians and lesbianism" by her partner's sibling. The exchange had a "profound impact" on them and made her acutely aware of her vulnerability should her partner die or become unwell. Legalization, for this participant, was a highly pragmatic response to a heightened sense of legal vulnerability that arose in the context of a family conflict over their sexuality: "So I just wanted that problem to go away, so that was my motivation to have a civil union which is extremely unromantic, very much based on that security of societal sanction."

As the legal rights gained through marriage become fewer than in the past, the celebration and partying that usually follows could easily be viewed as more important than the ceremony and change in legal status. In our study, several participants in different-sex and same-sex relationships reported that they had a brief legal ceremony with minimal witnesses, largely for practical reasons such as gaining legal rights for immigration, and then held a non-legal ceremony and celebration with friends and family which they called their "real wedding," even when it had no legal validity. These separate events were sometimes held in different countries or cities, and could be weeks or months apart. The celebratory event with family and friends was sometimes talked about as more important than the legal event, even though the couple valued the rights associated with marriage.

An example of a participant who had two "weddings" is a mother who cohabited for seven years with the father of her child before marrying. She contrasted their legal wedding, to which she had contemplated wearing jeans and jandals [flip-flops] and had not taken very seriously, with the "real" non-legal wedding to which she wore a formal custom-made dress:

In the District Court we got married. That was a bit of a laugh. . . .
I thought you just rocked up and signed a form but they actually

do a little ceremony. You have to say things to each other. I do remember standing there at one point and turning around and looking and everybody just looked so teary and I sort of thought, "gosh this is actually quite serious, we actually are getting married." So I wasn't even going to get changed and then just before we left everybody else had put on nice jeans and I was, "okay I suppose I should not wear my jandals to my wedding."

Later, she talked about her "real" wedding that was held the next day at a rustic camp in the bush, consisting of a community hall and bunkrooms:

The ceremony was conducted by a friend of mine who couldn't legally marry us so the ceremony was quite distinct from us getting legally married . . . "[Partner] didn't see my dress until I walked down the aisle, I mean there wasn't really an aisle, but until I walked in to where the ceremony was. . . . I did have to spend a bit of money on the dress, not thousands but hundreds. . . . It was just a beautiful celebration of our relationship and everything.

A gay couple in our study also legalized their relationship in a minimal manner at the local registry office and followed it few weeks later with a celebratory party where they announced their changed status to friends and family. However, this particular couple did not use the celebratory party as an occasion for a more elaborate wedding:

We both wore suits to the registry office, I think. We didn't buy anything specially. It was sort of like two o'clock in the afternoon or something so we both went to work for the morning and then my daughter was still at school at that point and so the four of us who'd been there and she, after she finished school, we just all met at the [x] Hotel for afternoon tea. And then we had a party about two or three weeks later when we told people what we'd done. Just invited people were here.

In jurisdictions such as New Zealand and Canada, marriage offers few additional legal protections over long-term cohabitation. In such a legal context, the significance of marriage is increasingly symbolic; it is linked to a change in the nature of commitment as well as the recognition afforded the couple. Thus, it is not surprising that couples focus on the celebratory and social aspects of getting married. However, because of the discrimination same-sex couples continue to face, they seem to be more attuned to the difficulties that can arise when partners are not recognized as next of kin. The sensitivity to this issue was particularly noticeable among the older same-sex couples in our study, no doubt a product of an increasing awareness of their own mortality but also of having lived through times that were much more overtly homophobic.

Expectations and Pressures to Marry

Many participants, both different- and same-sex, mentioned that getting married was considered the "normal" thing to do and had been part of their social upbringing or gender socialization since childhood. While some participants reported that they desired this kind of normal life course, others had resisted the social pressure or changed the order of expected life events, such as having a child before marrying, or marrying but remaining childless. For example, a young married woman under thirty years of age said: "Marriage was something I always wanted. You know, your little girl dreams as you're growing up, get married, get a house, have children. We're skipping the children part. We've got the house—my nice little white picket fence deal. My check boxes are checked." This woman seemed quite content to conform to traditional expectations of adulthood, although she seemed less invested in the idea of becoming a mother.

Some same-sex participants also talked about desiring a normal life course with marriage and children. For instance, a young lesbian woman who had recently had a civil union spoke of her expectations that she would one day marry, and her sadness at being debarred from that important life ritual:

Well I guess a little part of me has always thought that one day I would somehow get married. But I also knew that I couldn't because I was a lesbian . . . . So that was quite hard to face and when civil union came up I had these really mixed feelings about it. . . . But anyway I just kind of have always had that on my mind, that I wanted to commit to somebody in that kind of manner.

Similarly, a gay man in the throes of planning a civil union spoke of his long-term expectation that he would one day get married:

I think growing up I always wanted to be married and have a family and then I nearly did with [heterosexual ex-partner]. Well I did, I had a son. But then when that sort of broke down and I realized I was gay, I guess I was always still keen to meet someone who I would spend the rest of my life with.

As these comments suggest, same-sex couples are usually raised with similar social expectations about marriage and child-bearing. Yet once they "come out" and live openly with same-sex partners, they are seldom pressured to legalize their relationship with their same-sex partner, especially by their parents and older relatives. In fact, these couples sometimes decide to legalize despite opposition from "homophobic" relatives, as well as disapproval from some of their gay/lesbian friends who are antagonistic to the very idea of same-sex marriage. For example, the gay man mentioned above also spoke about his decision not to invite his parents to their wedding because:

My dad is pretty homophobic really. . . . We had an incident where I tried to introduce [partner]. We came around to my parents' place when we were in [city] and dad just walked out of the room. So, and then we had another conversation after that . . . with dad on the phone and he was saying things like "Well it's your life and if you want to throw it away" sort of thing. So I basically decided from that point on that I wasn't going to try. . . . And the reason I'm not inviting them to the wedding is because . . . I don't want them turning up on the day and completely ruining my day emotionally.

Another participant, a lesbian woman who entered a civil union with her long-term cohabiting partner, asked a friend to be a witness only to be confronted with her friend's antipathy toward civil unions: "She said no, she wouldn't be my witness, she wouldn't be a signatory, and that she would have nothing to do with civil unions. It was devastating . . . "

In contrast, some different-sex participants talked about resisting the social pressure to marry. For example, a highly educated male in his fifties, who had been contemplating a civil union with the mother of his child, talked about the pressure to marry: "All my brothers and sisters are married. It's kind of the thing to do. You grew up, left school, went to university, got an education, got a job and then you got married but I really wasn't having any of that." He went on to describe that he had been pressured by his mother, his female partner, and his school-aged child to formalize his cohabiting relationship. Often the pressure from parents to marry diminishes the longer the couple cohabits, which was implied by this man who had been cohabiting for fifteen years. He said: "I think my parents would rather have a proper wedding but I do really think they've finally given up and they'd be really happy to have even just a civil union. They're in their eighties now."

Other participants found the pressure to marry more difficult to resist, especially when it came from family and friends. The people we interviewed mentioned that parents generally expect their children to marry and that some parents cannot understand why their children would want to avoid or delay what they see as an important rite of passage. A female celebrant talked about the pressure in her family:

In my extended family there's one couple who lived together for ten to twelve years, got two children, and the family always said:

"when are you going to get married?" Well, he never wanted to but actually in the end they decided to and they just went to the registry office.

Several cohabitants reported that their mothers openly spoke of their desire for grandchildren but expected their son or daughter to marry first. Both celebrants and cohabitants agreed that many parents, older relatives, and cohabiting couples themselves believe that legal unions offer more secure environments in which to raise children. A male partner about to enter a different-sex civil union said that his mother was urging him to propose to his partner: "Definitely mum was sort of making the hints. I think she wants grandchildren, but that's probably not coming for a while." Although he reported that his mother was puzzled by his choice of civil union over marriage, she was pleased that he was legalizing his relationship before having children.

Celebrants also mentioned cases where children pressured their unmarried parents to formalize their relationship by continually asking them why they were not married. For example, a secular celebrant noted that this seemed to be the main motive to marry for two of her clients:

> I've had a couple that have always said to each other they would never get married but then they had children and the children started growing up and saying "why aren't you married? Blah-blah's mummy and daddy are married, why aren't you two married?" It can be the kids, you know, the pressure from their children.

A male participant who has been cohabiting for fifteen years also reported that his son seemed a bit concerned about their unmarried state:

> Every now and then [son] has this little concern about the fact that we're not married and why aren't we? He actually said to me

last week: "You realize, technically you're still dating" . . . And I say to him, "Why is it important to get married?" I think most of his classmates' parents would be married . . .

The celebrants also commented that the weddings of clients' friends sometimes encouraged them to marry, even when they were initially opposed to the idea or thought legal marriage was unnecessary. One celebrant commented: "As more people publicly celebrate their love in particular ways, the couples who have never wanted to get married because they thought being married meant x, go 'Oh! We can get married and it means what we want it to mean,' you know?" This comment suggests that creating personalized weddings with their own private meaning rather than relying on standardized ceremonies in religious or state venues could encourage some couples to marry. Indeed, Wallace (2004) argues that the appeal of the personalized wedding has been central to the survival of marriage as a social institution in the last thirty to forty years. The existence of personalized weddings seems to imply that marital relationships are just as susceptible to individual crafting as weddings have become.

Deciding to Formalize

Having the motive to marry is one thing, but actually taking concrete steps toward formalization is another. How did the couples in our study make the decision to legalize their relationships? The next section discusses three patterns from our interviews: marriage proposals, mutual decisions, and negotiated decisions, although some of these are overlapping rather than discrete categories.

Marriage Proposals

We were surprised that so many of our participants reported that their decision to formalize their relationship involved a marriage proposal by one partner, which seemed to overshadow any prior discussion they had and precipitated the public announcement of their "engagement." Among the different-sex couples, the marriage proposal normally came from the man, while in same-sex couples it usually came from the older partner. Some of these proposals were very elaborate romantic events, while others were more casual. For example, a young woman discussed how her male partner stage-managed a romantic proposal:

> It was a very long and drawn out day of extravaganza but the main part was we went to X Beach [north of Auckland] . . . . that's a place I used to go to a lot when I was growing up and he had had someone set up a picnic there for when we arrived because you have to walk around the rocks at low tide to get there. He went down on one knee and proposed and then we stayed at [expensive local hotel] that night.

Another young married woman talked about her male partner proposing in an unusually traditional way:

> I think there was an understanding between the both of us that we wanted to get married but at the same time [partner] did the whole kind of surprise engagement, ask my dad permission, blah, blah, blah. He kind of took the proactive step to initiate it actually happening, but there was an understanding that that was going to happen. It's not like he proposed and really wondered whether I was going to say yes or not. I think he knew.

Some different-sex participants seemed genuinely puzzled by their partner's desire for a formal proposal, such as this young woman who seemed to suggest that such a practice was outmoded:

> It was kind of funny. Like he really wanted to do like the traditional proposal that we'd already discussed, there wasn't much point for that but it was really important to him to do that. . . . Yeah we went out and looked at some engagement rings together and then he went back and chose one from the ones that we'd looked at. And then he sort of organized a surprise thing. . . . So

it was our five year anniversary I think and we went to a hotel in town and then he did this big romantic proposal over dinner with a guitarist and like he hired a personal classical guitarist and we were in this separated off area of the restaurant with like little curtains so they couldn't see us and then he did this big thing.

Other women expected and waited for the traditional male proposal, even though they had cohabited for many years, had previously discussed and agreed to marriage, and in some cases had already had a child together. For example, this highly educated woman in her forties said:

I guess it would have been a couple of years between us first talking about marriage and him finally getting around to proposing to me because . . . for reasons that I still do not understand, I wanted the whole you know down on the knee with the ring proposal and for it to be a surprise. So it would have been, I guess probably a full year before we decided we were going to get married and [partner] actually getting round to proposing to me.

One male participant proposed to his girlfriend twice before she agreed to marry. When the interviewer implied that he and his different-sex partner had mutually decided to marry, he corrected her: "No I proposed, of course, proposed twice, first time didn't work. I think she was a bit flabbergasted and hesitated two seconds too long to rescue the situation so that was it. So I had to ask again a few weeks later." This man felt confident that his partner wanted to marry but that she was simply surprised by the timing of his proposal, so he repeated it in a few weeks and she accepted. These examples show that some men and women still expect the man to propose marriage in different-sex relationships, and that some men go to considerable effort to stage-manage romantic and expensive proposals even when the couple has cohabited for years and previously discussed their intention to marry. Research from the United States also suggests that marriage proposals have remained the prerogative of men (Sassler and Miller 2011).

Not all proposals in our study were romantic. For example, a young married woman recounted the details of her husband's proposal:

> On New Year's Eve, we went to watch the fireworks at the Sky Tower . . . and my husband said: "Do you want to get married?" and I said "yes" and that was it. And everyone laughs when I say I don't remember a word of *how* he proposed. . . . I don't remember an inch of it because I was so drunk.

Another man spoke about a similarly unromantic proposal that took place at their home:

> We were just sitting on the couch and I asked her if she would marry me. It wasn't particularly romantic or a big event . . . . It was literally out of this one conversation that we were having and so she was saying that she was thinking of asking me for a while and . . . then I was like, "okay I'll ask her" and so I asked her. And she said "yes."

In our interviews, the proposals in the same-sex participants tended to come from the older partner. Here is a proposal story told by a woman under thirty who is one year older than her same-sex partner:

> I took her out for dinner and . . . by the time we finished it was still light . . . so I said "let's go for a drive up [volcanic peak in Auckland]." She said that she knew I was going to propose because I was acting weird, and I had the ring and I just said what I wanted to say to her and gave it to her just sitting in the car and she said yes. Even though I knew she was going to say yes it was

still pretty nerve wracking and then we came home and popped heaps of champagne and had a massive party and celebrated and started telling people straight away.

A gay man who is seven years older than his male partner told a similar story of a traditional proposal with a ring. However, this proposal took place while on an overseas vacation:

I just decided that I saw an opportunity, we were going away and I thought, yeah, so I sort of planned it for about six months to myself, kept it quiet, didn't tell anyone and yeah. Purchased the rings and planned it for when we were going over to [Asian holiday destination] . . . We went to [gay neighbours'] civil union a couple of years ago, just around the corner, and they've become good friends. I guess that is a slight influence. We've had a couple of friends that have had a civil union. So I guess that plays a little role.

The above example shows that same-sex couples can experience traditional "marriage" proposals and also that the ceremonies of friends can influence decisions to legalize their relationships. These examples also illustrate a finding from our research that the older same-sex partner was more likely to propose to the younger partner. However, this should be verified in future research.

Mutual Decisions

Many of our cohabiting participants talked about mutually deciding to formalize their relationship rather than experiencing a traditional marriage proposal without prior discussion. In particular, those heterosexual participants who valued gender equity, such as most of the partners in different-sex civil unions, shied away from conventional male proposals. These participants talked about the gradual development of relationship commitment over the years since they started to cohabit. For example, a young woman in a different-sex civil union said: "No, there wasn't really a proposal, I don't think. There was kind of a well, shall we? Okay let's. . . . I think it was me who said shall we. But it wasn't romantic." Another young married woman said:

> I think that we obviously were progressing towards a commit-
> ment in the sense that we combined our incomes well before we
> got engaged. . . . We also had a house before we got married. . . . I
> think we had talked about marriage at various points throughout
> our relationship. It was never a taboo topic. . . . We were always
> talking far in the future assuming that we would still be together.

Some of these so-called mutual decisions involved previous discussions in which one partner was more certain than the other about the desirability of marriage. In heterosexual relationships, it was often the woman who initially expressed the desire to formalize the relationship. A young male participant, now in a different-sex civil union, talked about the way they initially "decided" to cohabit: "That was actually probably a joint decision . . . it was practicalities really. We were just living out of each other's hand baskets and bathrooms. So we may as well combine the two. Yeah, that was definitely . . . a joint decision." He also reported that having a civil union was a mutual decision but further suggested that she was the "bossy one" in the couple:

> I'm not really a big family guy, or a big ceremony guy. So the whole
> thing of a wedding seems relatively, well essentially unnecessary
> is probably the best word there. . . . But it was obvious that [part-
> ner] wanted it and I definitely wanted to continue a relationship
> with [partner], because she's awesome. So it just sort of happened
> from there. After a few hints and after a few suggestions as to
> what rings looked nice on Trade Me[1] I went out hunting . . .

---

1. Trade Me is similar to eBay and is the major online auction house in New Zealand.

These comments suggest that mutual decisions to formalize relationships often required some discussion about the pros and cons, as well as the nature of the event. However, the idea was often initiated by the woman in heterosexual relationships and by the younger partner in same-sex relationships, even though an agreement to get married relied on the willingness of the more reticent partner, which was usually a heterosexual man or older same-sex partner.

Negotiated Decisions to Marry

Other cohabitants in our study reported that they had to manoeuvre their reluctant partner into proposing and/or agreeing to marry them. In different-sex relationships, this often involved eager women and reluctant men (see also Sassler and Miller 2011). For example, this recently remarried woman over sixty years old, who had been cohabiting with her male partner for thirteen years, said:

> At about maybe the five year mark . . . we started having conversations about marriage and when I say *we*, it's basically *me* because I'd say to him: "I really think we should get married. I'd really like to get married." And he'd say, "but why? What's going to change?" And he couldn't understand. "Convince me," you know, "that it's going to change . . ."

In the interview, she continued at length to describe her eight-year attempt to persuade her male partner to marry and her continuing quest, especially during vacations, for a conventional marriage proposal. During one such overseas vacation to North America, she made her regular pilgrimage to a favourite silversmith, initially with thoughts of buying a bracelet but eventually settling on a carved ring, which to her surprise her partner offered to buy. About an hour later, he casually proposed. Here is the last part of her long proposal story:

> We were driving on this lovely road . . . in the mountains . . . and we were talking about lots of other stuff and [the proposal] was

like an interjection almost. And then we continued to talk about other stuff, and you know, I said to him, "did you just ask me to marry you?" And I said "okay, we'll have to sort that out." And then, "that sounds good [partner's name], like how many years has it been?"

Another reluctant male cohabitant was persuaded by his long-term female partner to propose marriage through cue cards she had made for him to use during the noisy helicopter ride to his fortieth birthday celebrations on a nearby island. Here is part of her story:

I was thinking how am I going to get [partner] to propose to me? . . . . You've got to have some old-fashionedness about it, even though I'm controlling it. . . . Conniving woman. He didn't stand a chance. I'm the cat going in for the kill now. . . . I know how I'm going to do it, we're in the helicopter, I'm going to give him the cards with the words on it to read to me. . . . So I wrote the cards out and I said please read these cards. The next one said "I love you lots." The next one said, "will you marry me?" And then I had one that said, "yes." Then I had one ready that said, "you've got ten seconds, if you don't propose to me I'll propose to you . . . " I felt sick. I was so nervous. It was just like being the bloke, propos- ing. . . . So he goes okay, "I love you lots, will you marry me?" And I went "yes." And we both went, "shit." I went, "Oh! I guess we're engaged then." It was quite nerve racking but it was exciting as well. . . . So that was really cool. So that's how I cornered him into proposing to me. I thought that was genius.

This woman actually persuaded him to propose twice, to ensure that he really agreed to go through with the wedding after eight years of cohabitation.

Younger participants also provided stories of negotiated "pro- posals." For example, a married woman under thirty years old told a shorter version of the reluctant male who is persuaded to become "engaged" after four years of cohabiting:

[My partner] had decided . . . to get a motorcycle as we needed a second vehicle. . . . We could afford it but we thought it would be easier for us to get a loan just to tide us over so that we weren't scrimping. We only needed about $2,000 but the minimum bank loan was $5,000. So I said, [in front of the bank officer] "If you get a bike, I get a ring," and he said, "okay." And then when we got home, I asked him again if he really meant it and he said yes, and we were engaged.

Her male partner's version of the same story (told in a separate interview) emphasized his belief that legal marriage was unnecessary and his embarrassment over the bank loan incident. He reported the additional information that she sent text messages to their friends within thirty minutes of the "proposal." When friends sent their congratulations, he reported he felt that he had no other option than to "go through with it." However, he later spoke with some ambivalence about the situation and implied that he felt lucky to avoid making a formal proposal since he couldn't rule out the potential that she might have refused him:

You just hear horror stories, like guys who have asked *the question*, you hear some really wonderful stories, but you hear some real horror stories. So yeah, I feel quite lucky that I didn't have to put my relationship to the test by having asked someone the question that they might say no to. . . . I almost got married against my will. It was awesome. I mean I'm so happy.

Among the same-sex couples in our study, one partner sometimes wanted a commitment ceremony or legal union before the other, something they held in common with some of our different-sex participants. For example a woman told a story of the day that her older female partner finally agreed to have a same-sex civil union, after seventeen years of cohabitation and many of her prior suggestions to have a commitment ceremony. Although she told us that her partner saw civil union as "heterosexist and patriarchal," she finally agreed to legalize to help clarify the nature of their relationship with the younger woman's homophobic family:

> For years I'd wanted some kind of ceremony, not for . . . reasons around legality necessarily but yeah, for my own wanting to celebrate the relationship, which I am and have been extremely happy about for many years. . . . I'd asked [older partner] earlier about a commitment ceremony and she didn't want that. . . . I think she was essentially very shy and didn't want a big public thing. But after this conversation in the car [about my family's objection to our sexual preference], as we were driving to [another city in New Zealand], she was the one that initiated it.

Not all participants who reported that they had decided to marry had actually made concrete plans for their wedding. A woman in her late fifties, who had been cohabiting with her male partner for over twelve years, referred to herself as "engaged" and was wearing an engagement ring during the interview. When the interviewer asked about it, she answered: "It's a commitment ring, he said. So he's committed, and that's what it is . . . . but is he really ready to commit? . . . There was never any proposal . . . ." She continued to tell the story of buying the ring:

> We were in Michael Hill [jewellery store] and I was looking in the dress ring cabinet and he was behind me and he said "Why don't we look over here?," which was the engagement ring cabinet. He said, "What about that one?" and I looked at him and sort of thought, what's going on here but didn't say anything except "Oh, that one is really nice." So tried it on and yes we bought it.

She repeated that there was never any proposal and pretended to be speaking for her male partner: "Will I, won't I, do I, don't I? I don't want to get married but I want to be committed." Another man mentioned an agreement in principle to enter a civil union with his different-sex partner of fifteen years in similarly open and vague terms: "We have discussed a civil union several times since it became an option and we were going to do it once I got the [university degree] but life kind of got in the way, so she's just had her fiftieth birthday and we've just started talking about it again."

These stories are only a few from our interviews but they are consistent with overseas research findings that males typically retain more control over heterosexual relationship changes despite other improvements in women's status (Sassler and Miller 2011). These comments from our participants also suggest that the transition to formalization, which can involve considerable time and negotiation, is not always equally valued by both partners. In fact, agreeing in principle to the idea of engagement or marriage can be used, in some cases, as a strategy to further delay the actual wedding date.

Opposing Heterosexual Marriage by Choosing Civil Union

In Chapter 1, we noted that two forms of legalization existed in New Zealand and the United Kingdom at the time of our study, and two forms still exist in some American and Australian states. When we completed our interviews in New Zealand, same-sex couples were only permitted to enter civil unions while different-sex couples had a choice between civil union and marriage. However, government statistics indicate that the vast majority of heterosexual couples who formalized their relationships (99.6 percent) chose marriage. In our interviews, we over-sampled different-sex participants entering civil unions because the reasons they choose this form of legalization are not well understood. Five out of forty participants, or eight percent of our sample, were in the category of different-sex civil unions. Their reasons for choosing civil union over marriage were not always clearly articulated, although they typically viewed civil unions as more inclusive and less associated with organized religion and traditional gender roles. For example, one woman explained her choice of civil union as a way of opposing marriage, which she saw as a gendered institution:

I've always been very opposed to marriage. My mother who is, as far as I can tell quite happily married to my father and they've been married for like forty years or something bizarre, has always instilled to me that marriage is an institution designed for the suppression of women and that I should avoid it, blah, blah, blah, just that kind of seventies feminist aversion. But I don't think I would ever have got married, but civil union kind of gave us an opportunity to have a. . . . We had been thinking about having a party. We were going to call it an "entanglement." This was well before the civil union legislation was passed. We wanted to do something to kind of say yeah. [Partner's] parents are very old-fashioned and were devastated that we were showing no signs of getting married. So it was kind of nice.

This woman felt that having a civil union showed her opposition to traditional gendered marriage. She did not elaborate on how marriage was oppressive to women or why she thought that civil union would be different, yet she reported that marriage had negative connotations for her.

Her male partner, who was interviewed separately, acknowledged that she had no faith in the institution of marriage. Nevertheless, he felt that *he* wanted to make some form of public commitment:

[My partner] grew up in a family where marriage was like a bad thing. . . . One of her first sentences [to me] was: "Marriage is an institution designed for the suppression of women," so I didn't think we were ever going to get married. . . . However I felt like you need some way to signal to other people that it's . . . not just kind of like this is my girlfriend. But we never had any intention of getting married . . . and we thought it would be really nice to have a big party. Have some kind of celebration but that was kind as far as it ever got. So when the civil union legislation was passed, it was like that would be a way to do this which avoids all of those problems.

This man continued to say: "I think an aspect of our civil union was kind of like a public vote of confidence in that legislation. . . . I think it's more just a declaration of your own . . . political viewpoint as much as anything." Again, he did not articulate how or why a civil union would be less objectionable than marriage to him or to his female partner.

The participants who entered into different-sex civil unions also mentioned that they had to carefully explain to family and friends why they were making this unorthodox choice. For example, a young woman who was about to enter a different-sex civil union said that her mother was happy about her decision to formalize and not bothered by her decision to have a civil union but her partner's family had some concerns: "His parents were really happy that we were forming a union and then they found out it was a civil union and they just had a lot of questions around it and we talked to them about it. They've been really supportive after we had that conversation." This young woman's partner, whose mother had been pressuring him to provide her with grandchildren, talked about her response to his announcement of the civil union:

> I think my mother was surprised because she thought that civil union was just for gays. I say that because my parents are incredibly old-fashioned. My father is racist, sexist, everything. . . . I went to get a will done, and the lawyer said to me your mum was very interested in the difference between civil unions and marriages last time they came in. . . . So she was obviously sussing out the legalities of it. . . . But once she realized that it was the same as marriage . . . she was real sweet with it.

If participants are aware that civil union is legally similar to marriage, as is suggested by the quote above, why would they feel that legalizing their relationship with a civil union would avoid the historical problems of traditional marriage? This question was not adequately answered by the participants in our study but the different-sex participants who were entering into civil unions seemed to view themselves as pioneers who were promoting new inclusive legislation or making oppositional statements about the old-fashioned institution of marriage. In doing so, they were often faced with a barrage of questions from family and friends about their non-normative choice of formalization. It seemed that family and friends were unsure about the legal ramifications of a civil union, and some saw it as a special arrangement for same-sex couples. However, another perspective about the differences between the two types of legalization became more apparent in the interviews with same-sex partners, who form the majority of civil unions. These participations often faced much more serious opposition from family and friends.

Same-Sex Civil Union as Second-Class Marriage

Several celebrants in our study discussed the significance of the socio-legal change that took place in 2004 when the New Zealand Parliament permitted the legalization of same-sex relationships. One female celebrant said: "For entire generations of same-sex couples, this is not something you'd ever considered as part of your future. And suddenly it's there and that's actually quite a shift in headspace." Another older female celebrant made a similar comment:

> I think same-sex couples put more time into their ceremonies than heterosexuals do and I think that's to do with the fact that it's very new and they've been prevented in the past from this and there's often political stuff that needs to be expressed about their relationships as well, which heterosexual couples don't need.

Participants further argued that status differences remain between the two forms of legal union in New Zealand. Somewhat surprisingly, the three male ministers of religion in our study particularly struggled with the "exclusive" nature of marriage. For example, a young heterosexual minister who only presides over marriages because his church opposes same-sex civil unions seemed concerned about his own moral position when he said:

I had someone who really challenged me a few weeks ago saying "why do I continue to support an unjust structure in marriage, because it's exclusive, whereas there's the alternative of civil union, which is inclusive?" I had to say, "yeah, I'd continue to think on that." . . . I sort of thought we've got that problem solved because we've got an alternative and it's got some more status. Her argument was, "but then why are so many more couples continuing to get married?" Her argument is because marriage has much higher social status.

An older gay minister whose church permits him to perform civil unions as well as marriages expressed a similar viewpoint more strongly when he said: "In some ways, the civil union option feels like a kind of a second-class wedding, second-class marriage. On the other hand, any legal recognition is better than no legal recognition." He continued to say that he saw no reason why same-sex couples would want to legalize their unions in a patriarchal and homophobic church, even though his own church permitted it: "Gay men and lesbians wanting a civil union, if they've had any experience of the church, they've usually had a bad experience. Why would they go into a system which has abused them to celebrate their relationship?" To some extent his comments are borne out by the fact that the vast majority of civil unions are celebrated in secular venues, as are most marriages. However, should same-sex couples want a church ceremony, their way is often barred because a number of religious congregations still refuse to accept same-sex civil unions.

Many same-sex cohabitants we interviewed also viewed civil union as "second-class marriage" but at the same time, they were grateful that the legislation had been passed. One young lesbian woman, who recently had a civil union before a large group of relatives and friends, discussed her ambivalence about the two categories of "marriage":

I feel like civil union is a little bit second class. It's kind of like saying we don't want you to get married because you're not really like a good enough citizen to be married, but we're going to give you this as some kind of second prize kind of way. . . . But on the other hand, I also feel like perhaps I don't want to assimilate myself with heterosexual people in terms of being married. . . . So yeah there are these two kinds of tensions. . . . People say things like: "Oh well, civil union is the same as marriage." And I always say to those people: "No it's not the same! Our relationships aren't necessarily recognized overseas, for instance, whereas yours are!"

Later in the interview, this woman spoke of placing her "wedding" photos on Facebook and her surprise and anger that they generated insulting and homophobic comments from strangers.

An older man in a same-sex civil union also expressed mixed feelings about civil unions, which was typical of the same-sex participants: "I still struggle with the fact that gay people can't access marriage . . . civil union appeals to me because it seems inherently equal." He also praised the "extraordinary" social change surrounding same-sex relationships in one generation:

I suppose for somebody in their early fifties, a remarkable journey of growing up gay and not being able to talk about it in the family to a point where you could be standing in the registry office having a civil union in one lifetime is just extraordinary. That was the greatest pleasure, realizing my rights.

Same-sex participants agreed that the opportunity to legalize their relationships was a big step forward for same-sex couples, although they also mentioned that this opportunity was not always understood or appreciated by their family and friends. For instance, a young woman mentioned that the initial announcement of her intentions to have a same-sex civil union generated family problems, although these were later resolved:

My family are Catholic. There's quite a lot of church in their background and mum reacted really badly about the civil union. . . .

When you're a lesbian and you look straight like I do, no one even really thinks that you're gay. . . . I think those thoughts were going through her mind, like she can't hide it any longer from other people.

Other same-sex participants mentioned that their parents did not know how to react when they announced their forthcoming union. For example, one "engaged" woman said: "It's one thing when you've got a child who is gay or a lesbian but it's another thing for them to get married I think. It's the two sort of acceptance things."

In addition, several participants talked about disagreements within the gay/lesbian communities about the wisdom of civil unions. This sometimes involved opposition to monogamy or the so-called mimicking of heterosexual relationships, or the belief that the state had no role in personal choices about intimate relationships. A same-sex celebrant said:

There are people in the gay/lesbian community who are very clearly *not* supporters of civil unions and that's fine. It's entirely their right . . . but then when their friends want to have a civil union, they then have to choose whether or not to come. I mean your friends don't tend to say, "No I can't come to your wedding because I don't support marriage."

Some same-sex participants in our study expected, but did not always receive, support from their gay and lesbian friends. As noted earlier in this book, one woman invited her lesbian friend to become her bridesmaid/witness but the friend refused, saying that she wanted nothing to do with civil unions. However, some stories also suggested unanticipated levels of acceptance by relatives and heterosexual colleagues.

Conclusions

Both the wider research and our interviews suggest that the reasons are varied for formalizing long-term cohabiting relationships, but most couples want to express their love and commitment in a public way, make a statement about the permanence of their relationship, and celebrate their "successful" relationship with family and friends. Our interviews showed little difference between the reported motives of same-sex and different-sex couples, although same-sex couples tended to place greater emphasis on the importance of gaining legal protections, the acceptance by kin, and acknowledgement and respect for their relationship. This has also been found in British and American studies (Schecter et al. 2008; Shipman and Smart 2007).

In our interviews, the portion of straight participants choosing civil union over marriage was admittedly small but these participants seemed to believe—rightly or wrongly—that civil unions are more inclusive and egalitarian, and less religious. Many of these participants mutually decided to marry, without a male marriage proposal, and none of the women changed their surname. Clearly, civil unions are more inclusive of sexual preference but there is little research evidence to date to suggest that years after the ceremony, different-sex civil unions are actually more egalitarian than marriages. Nevertheless, several of the participants seeking different-sex civil unions seemed to value gender equity.

There is a long tradition of civil marriage ceremonies in English-speaking countries, and only a minority of couples in countries like Australia and New Zealand now marry in places of worship. Secular celebrants have been marrying couples outside churches for decades and these ceremonies need not contain any mention of God or religion, or any reference to a gendered division of labour. As we will see in Chapter 4, wedding ceremonies in New Zealand and Australia are increasingly secular and personalized affairs, and most couples expect to incorporate their own values and personalities into their ceremonies, with some guidance from their celebrants. However, the connotations of marriage as an unequal, religious, and exclusive institution remain important for the different-sex couples entering civil unions.

The cultural dominance of marriage combined with the

newness of same-sex unions mean that gay and lesbian couples sometimes adopt the language and some of the symbols associated with heterosexual marriage. Even when same-sex couples enter into civil unions or civil partnerships they sometimes experience romantic proposals and speak about being engaged. Despite the legal similarities and the fact that ceremonies and celebrations can be indistinguishable, as we will see later in this book, the social context of same-sex civil unions remains different from heterosexual marriage.

The decision to marry by heterosexuals is generally viewed as a normal stage in the life cycle and an opportunity for celebration, even though marriage rates have been declining for decades. For same-sex couples, the decision to legalize their relationship is sometimes greeted with bafflement or even opposition from family and friends, even friends within the gay and lesbian communities. In the next chapter, we examine aspects of the "wedding industry" and its impact on the style and cost of weddings.

CHAPTER 3

"Proper" Weddings and the Wedding Industry

Introduction

Current weddings tend to be more elaborate and expensive than in previous decades (Boden 2003; Ingraham 2008; Otnes and Pleck 2003). Social research suggests that more heterosexual couples now postpone marriage until they have sufficient savings to afford a "real wedding" that satisfies their dreams and/or signifies their actual or desired socio-economic status (Cherlin 2004; Smock et al. 2005). This chapter focuses on changing social expectations of marriage and weddings, including the influence of the "wedding industry" or the many businesses that make money from these events. These include wedding consultants, bridal shops and magazines, wedding shows and exhibitions, independent marriage celebrants, and commercial wedding venues. We investigate how this industry, along with representations of weddings in popular culture and the social expectations of friends and family, help to shape prevalent ideas about "proper" weddings, including their style and average cost. We believe that a deeper understanding of the commercialization and personalization of weddings can contribute to the sociological analysis of the rise of a consumer-oriented and individualistic society.

Clearly, the social expectations and legal requirements of marriage have changed over the decades. Marriage used to be a patriarchal and exclusively heterosexual "institution" headed by the man, with gendered roles and expectations defined initially by the church and then later by the state, but widely promoted by families and communities. Following extensive criticism of patriarchal marriage by women's rights activists in the late nineteenth century, and later by second-wave feminists in the 1970s, marriage has become more egalitarian but also more diverse. While some heterosexual couples, usually those with a strong religious affiliation, continue to opt for a more conventional marriage, many secular couples and those with higher education tend to pursue more egalitarian relationships that are characterized by higher expectations of role negotiation, if not higher levels of equal roles or decision-making power. In some places, political agitation by same-sex activists means that marriage is no longer an exclusively heterosexual institution.

Legal marriage has also become more open to negotiation and personalization, slightly easier to enter, and much easier to leave. Rather than a tie that binds irrevocably, marriage is increasingly viewed as a personal living arrangement based on mutual satisfaction and happiness. In other words, the longevity of marriage is increasingly based on a couple's ongoing desire to be together, rather than on the various obstacles (such as social disapproval) that might prevent them from parting company, even though the influence of such obstacles has not completely dissipated. This view represents a substantial divergence from the meaning of marriage prevalent in the nineteenth and early twentieth centuries, as we see in the next section.

Changing Views of Marriage

In early Christian doctrine, the status of marriage was elevated from a private contract between individuals to a religious sacrament presided over by the church that was deemed to be indissoluble except by death (Fletcher 1973). By the nineteenth century, the state had become more involved by specifying who was legally entitled to marry, by requiring potential brides and grooms to obtain a licence from state authorities, and by keeping official records of legal marriages, although records were also retained by individual churches. Historically, both the church and state in the English-speaking countries viewed marriage as an economic and sexual partnership between husbands and wives that involved mutual dependency in the common endeavours of earning a living and raising children (Funder and Harrison 1993; Baker 2010). Until the early twentieth century, marriage played a vital role in the economic and social survival of both men and women, although marriage rates tended to fluctuate with economic conditions, opportunities to find partners, and legal requirements.

The roots of current marriage laws are found in common law in the English-speaking jurisdictions, while the civil code provides the basis for family law in the Canadian province of Quebec and much of Western Europe (Baker 2010). In both forms of law, the marital rights and responsibilities of men and women used to differ. The husband/father was considered to be the head of the household and was entitled to make the major household decisions on behalf of his wife and children. Husbands, for example, retained the right to establish the couple's legal residence or "domicile" but were expected to provide their wives with the "necessaries of life," although husbands also had the right to decide what was "necessary" well into the middle of the twentieth century (Dranoff 1977: 25).

Until the nineteenth and early twentieth centuries, husbands also controlled their wives' income and property, voted on their behalf, and retained guardianship of any children resulting from the marriage. In contrast, a wife was expected to live wherever her husband chose to live, to maintain their household, care for their children, and be sexually available when he wanted. Nevertheless, in recognition of these services, she was entitled to his financial support and to "dower rights" or the right to one-third of his property under common law should the marriage dissolve.[1]

---

1.   These legally sanctioned inequalities were the target of first-wave feminist activism, which is perhaps best remembered for its campaigns for female suffrage. Women gained the legal right to vote in national elections in New Zealand in 1893, in Australia in 1902, in Canada in 1918, in the United States in 1920 and 1928 in the United Kingdom. However, in the Canadian province of Quebec, married women were not permitted to vote in provincial elections until 1940 or to become the legal guardians of their own children until 1964 (Baker 2001: 183; Dranoff 1977: 39).

Despite these stark gendered inequalities, marriage was considered to be an important rite of passage, or a significant symbol of maturity, heterosexuality, and adulthood, and both women and men expected to marry. Men typically proposed marriage to women when they were financially and emotionally in a position to marry, and were expected to seek the consent of the bride's father. The couple normally cemented their legally binding agreement to marry with a public announcement, a family celebration, and from post–World War I onward, increasingly with an expensive engagement ring which he gave to her, serving as a symbol to other men that she was "taken."

Historically the engagement period was an important transitional phase for the couple that served a number of purposes (Otnes and Pleck 2003). First, it permitted the engaged couple to become more intimately acquainted with each other and with their respective families. Second, it enabled the husband-to-be to develop a secure source of income and to put aside money in order for the couple to acquire an independent residence. Third, it afforded wives-to-be the necessary time to stock their trousseaus or "bundles" with important household items, including bedding, linen, pots and pans, china, and the like.

According to Otnes and Pleck (2003), the prominent global magazine called *Brides* has steadily increased the recommended wedding preparation period from a mere two months in the late 1950s, to six months in the 1970s and 1980s, and to twelve or more months in the 1990s and 2000s. The increase in wedding preparation time coincides with the rise of premarital cohabitation, a phenomenon that one might have expected to shorten the engagement period since cohabiting couples have "already acquired the goods necessary for setting up a household" (ibid: 60). Yet as Otnes and Pleck explain, contemporary couples require " . . . enough time for the wedding and honeymoon to be meticulously planned so the couple may revel in romance, magic, memories, and perfection" (ibid: 61).

As befitted its definition as a religious sacrament, a wedding typically took place in a church or other place of worship. Churches tend to be monumental buildings that lend formality and dignity to the proceedings, and mark the event as one of great significance to the couple and their families. It was customary in most "white weddings" for the bride to be walked up the aisle by her father and given away by him to the groom at the altar. Prior to the 1960s, a bride typically promised to "love, honour, and obey" her husband, while the groom promised to "love, honour, and cherish" his wife (Baker 2001: 186). Such practices reflected the historical patriarchal nature of marriage, although variations in ceremonies have always been apparent by jurisdiction, culture, and religion.

Since the 1970s, governments have extended the same rights and responsibilities to wives and husbands in most cases, making family law more "gender neutral." These legal changes reflect public pressure for greater equality for women and men within many aspects of life, as well as more opportunities for interpersonal negotiation within marriage. In the past decade, same-sex couples have gained the right to legalize their relationships in a number of jurisdictions. This was done either by making marriage more inclusive (as in Canada, but now also in New Zealand) or creating a new non-religious legal arrangement called civil union/partnership (as in the Australian state of Queensland and the Australian Capital Territory, and initially in New Zealand and the United Kingdom). Some governments, such as Canada and New Zealand, have also treated cohabitants largely like married couples after they have lived together for a certain number of years.

Public attitudes have also changed and both governments and churches have modified their rules and practices about marriage and wedding ceremonies. All of the English-speaking countries have certified judges, justices of the peace, or clerks of the court to carry out official marriage ceremonies, and many have also legalized marriage commissioners or celebrants in the last forty years, largely as a result of increasing secularization. As a consequence, many couples are now married outside a church or registry office, especially in New Zealand and in Australia, England, and Wales (where civil ceremonies now account for about two-thirds of all marriages). Interestingly, Canadian statistics from 2001 (the most recent available) indicate that clergy officiated at 82 percent of first marriages but only 66 percent of remarriages (VIF 2004: 31).

These changes have paved the way for weddings to become occasions for personalization, celebrations of romance, and events of conspicuous consumption (Boden 2003; Cherlin 2004; Otnes and Pleck 2003). The white wedding gown occupies a pivotal place in modern consumerist weddings—it is usually the focal point of the bride's long-held fantasies for the day, as well as the centrepiece of the wedding spectacle. Supposedly laced with "talismanic power," the white wedding dress promises brides-to-be a transcendent experience by transforming them into princesses for one day (Otnes and Pleck 2003). Since the 1930s three norms have governed decisions about the wedding gown: "it should be white [or cream], it should be worn only once in a woman's lifetime and it should be a fashion statement all its own . . . " (ibid: 41).

Despite the rise of the secular, lavish consumerist wedding, marriage remains an important life event that signifies maturity, responsibility, legitimacy, and public commitment (Cherlin 2004). Canadian survey research by Reginald Bibby (2004) found that 90 percent of teens aged fifteen to nineteen expect to get married at some point in their life, and 88 percent reported that they expected to remain with the same partner for life. As we might assume, these figures fall dramatically with age and vary by region. Bibby also found that 93 percent of Canadian respondents believed that marriage signifies relationship commitment.

A 2005 Australian survey of over ten thousand people aged fifteen and over also explored attitudes toward marriage and cohabitation (Qu and Weston 2008a). It found widespread rejection of the notion that marriage is an outdated social institution. Unsurprisingly, young people under the age of thirty were less likely to disagree with this notion than people older than sixty years of age. Similarly, young people under thirty were more likely to approve of cohabitation even if couples have no intentions to marry. Interestingly, two-thirds or more of those aged between forty and fifty-nine also approved of unmarried cohabitation without any intention to marry, suggesting that most parents of Australian young people are unlikely to apply pressure on their children to marry. Likewise, cross-national research on attitudes to marriage indicates continued widespread support for marriage as an institution among those living in Europe, the United Kingdom and in the United States (Scott 2006; Pongracz and Spéder 2008).

Same-sex marriages represent the latest change in the nature of the institution of marriage. The campaign for same-sex marriage rights began in the 1980s but reached critical mass in the English-speaking countries in the early 2000s. As we've noted elsewhere, Canada has legalized same-sex marriage (as has New Zealand in April 2013), but both the United Kingdom and New Zealand previously created new legal institutions—civil partnerships in the United Kingdom and civil unions in New Zealand—which accorded same-sex couples similar rights to their married counterparts. However, the legal recognition of same-sex relationships has not always translated into the right to get married in a church. Indeed, in most cases, same-sex couples have no choice but to get married in a registry office or in a civil ceremony officiated by a secular celebrant.

Many private companies have taken advantage of the continued importance attached to marriage, of the legal changes permitting marriages to be solemnized in new locations, and of the increasing desire for individualized weddings by offering to help couples plan elaborate, unique, exotic, romantic, and expensive events. The next section examines the current marriage and wedding imagery that is prevalent in popular culture, and what it represents.

Popular Culture and Wedding Imagery

Wedding imagery is pervasive in popular culture. The weddings of celebrities and royalty frequent the covers of women's magazines, daily newspapers, and television news. In 2005 Elton John's wedding to his long-term partner, David Furnish, was big news, not only because of their celebrity status, but also because they were one of the first gay couples to take advantage of the legalization of civil partnerships in the United Kingdom. More recently the wedding of Prince William and Catherine Middleton in the United Kingdom, like the wedding of Prince Charles and Diana Spencer thirty years before, was also the subject of intense media speculation prior to the event, and was broadcast on radio, television, and the Internet to a global audience of tens of millions of people. Brides and weddings have served, and continue to serve, as the focal point for hundreds of films and television shows (Ingraham 2008). In addition, glossy wedding magazines, which relay stories about ordinary and celebrity weddings and offer brides-to-be advice on how to plan for their "big day," have come to occupy a significant foothold in the women's magazine market (Boden 2003; Husbands 2006). All of these portrayals play a pivotal role in shaping social expectations about the nature of "real weddings" and what they represent (Boden 2003; Ingraham 2008).

One feature of wedding culture that academic researchers have observed is the continued link to "hetero-normativity," or the idea that it is male–female intimate relationships that deserve public celebration and recognition through wedding ceremonies. Associations have also been perceived between the imagery surrounding brides and cultural ideals of femininity (Ingraham 2008; Tombaugh 2009). The picture-perfect bride remains a powerful representation of "ultimate femininity" (Boden 2003). However, the links between gender and weddings are not confined to matters of appearance. Researchers have documented that when wedding planning is done within the family, it continues to be a gendered activity for which the bride is usually seen to be responsible, along with her mother and sisters (Humble et al. 2008; Sniezek 2005).

The wedding industry includes exhibitions and fashion shows, jewellery stores selling engagement and wedding rings, wedding shops selling or renting white/ivory gowns and tuxedos, glossy magazines displaying fashionable weddings, planners paid to organize all aspects of weddings, and secular celebrants who preside over ceremonies but also encourage certain wedding practices.

Furthermore, this industry includes the rising number of commercial venues, such as historic houses, vineyards, and resorts, which help to organize and host these events.

Ostensibly, the wedding industry serves the needs of different-sex couples but in reality it primarily targets brides-to-be as potential consumers of their services, promising to make their dreams for their wedding day a reality. As Blakely (2008) argues with respect to the relatively recent development of the wedding planning industry, the language of liberal feminism has been co-opted, along with the ideal of "having it all," to encourage busy professional women to outsource more of their wedding planning. Thus work that was traditionally done by the bride and to a lesser extent her female family members has become a fee-paying service delivered by unrelated women.

Following the emergence of same-sex weddings or same-sex civil partnerships, the wedding industry has expanded, both creating and accommodating demands among gay and lesbian couples. These couples can consult speciality websites (for example, http://equallywed.com), attend specialty wedding expos and fairs, hire the services of specialty wedding planners (for instance, "love, honor and be gay" at http://www.lhbgay.com), and consult speciality celebrants or officiators, all of which form part of the growing "pink" wedding industry. In New York alone, it is estimated that same-sex weddings will lead to a growth of up to $100 million (US) for the wedding industry (Williams 2012). In the United Kingdom, it would seem that same-sex couples are willing to pay more than different-sex couples for their weddings, with the average spend for same-sex couples being about £4,000 (over $6,000 Canadian) more than different-sex couples (Matheson 2006).

Before interacting with various elements of the wedding industry, couples who have decided to marry, especially heterosexual women, typically discuss their wedding plans with friends and family, seeking advice about suitable venues, types of events, and celebrants. Increasingly, couples turn to websites for further information, including those from government departments, wedding planners, celebrant organizations, independent celebrants, and churches. These websites provide future brides and grooms (as members of different- or same-sex couples) with considerable information about the legal requirements for "marriage," various options for the wording of ceremonies and vows, the fees charged by celebrants or venues, and other planning considerations. But these websites, as well as bridal magazines and shows, are not simply sources of information; like the weddings of celebrities and royalty, they also generate criteria against which people judge whether a wedding has been successful, and thereby act as an important source of influence.

In our study, we used marriage celebrants as key informants not only because they are aware of current wedding trends but also because discussions with their clients usually include their motives for marrying and details about clients' personal circumstances. Couples may initially email or telephone their chosen celebrant to discuss their wedding plans, but they also typically arrange at least one face-to-face meeting to discuss further details. In some cases, couples and celebrants exchange numerous emails and phone calls, and meet on several occasions to fine-tune these details. In our study, we also asked the long-term cohabitants to tell us about their wedding or wedding plans. This often led to detailed descriptions of the venue, the number of guests, the role of various participants, the readings or speeches included in the ceremony, the clothing they wore, the reception and honeymoon, and conflicts or problems surrounding the event.

Several celebrants talked about the assumptions of normality and maturity associated with heterosexual marriage and the importance of weddings as indicators of success for females. One female celebrant said: "Some women come to me with a folder this big of cut-outs they've had since they were like three and they know exactly how their wedding is going to go. And it seems like they just kind of found the guy to fit into that folder. . . . For some, it's very much about the external: 'I'm married, I have succeeded . . . '" The link between marriage and women's success is an age-old connection, reinforced by the low status of the nineteenth-century "spinster"[2] and related derogatory expressions about unmarried women living alone, such as being "on the shelf." In addition, most women are better off financially when living with a male partner than when living alone, as acquiring a male household income usually raises women's living standards, which then elevates their status among their peers.

A few participants mentioned that their ideas about weddings or those of their partner had been influenced by celebrity or royal weddings, or weddings they saw on television. For example, one young woman in her twenties, about to enter a same-sex civil union, mentioned the discussions she had with her female partner about their wedding:

> We talked about wanting a small intimate ceremony on the beach. And [partner] was all for it and then she changed her mind and she doesn't want that anymore. And that's cool. It was interesting, we were watching the royal wedding on television and [partner] was like: "I want to be that person, I like that grandiose." So hopefully we'll be able to find a happy medium.

In a separate interview, her lesbian partner speculated about the dress she would wear to her wedding: "I want something not so white and fluffy and things. I like the look of, you know the royal wedding, the maid of honour, what was her name? She had a nice sort of, it was probably silk, but it was nice and straight and came down to her feet, something like that, straps and things." In fact, several female participants mentioned the royal wedding between Prince William and Catherine Middleton, which was shown on television in 2011, just before our interviews.

Although reading about fashionable weddings in magazines or watching royal weddings on television could motivate couples to create more elaborate celebrations for their own wedding, a married

---

2.   Although spinsters or unmarried women held a low status, they retained many legal and political rights denied to women upon marriage.

woman in our study suggested that the media also encouraged couples to delay their weddings: "There is all that kind of popular culture, social media stuff about finding the perfect relationship and the perfect this and perfect that. . . . So I think a lot of people wait because they're looking for that idealized version of love." These comments suggest that the media can have multiple influences on the timing and nature of wedding ceremonies and celebrations.

The Retention of Wedding Traditions

Weddings have always been highly symbolic events, even though the symbols and their meanings have changed over time. In Western countries the symbolism has focused on the union of two families, the couple's lifetime commitment, the expectation of fertility and child-rearing within marriage, the beginning of a new generation, and, more recently, romance and eternal love. Patriarchal symbols have occupied, and in many cases continue to occupy, a prominent place: women typically wear engagement rings to indicate that they are "taken," brides are "given away" as if they are possessions to the groom by their father, and women often take their husband's surname after marriage in keeping with the historical absorption of a woman's legal status within that of her husband. The white dress, which became fashionable following Queen Victoria's marriage to Prince Albert in 1840, symbolizes the historical expectation of the bride's virginity, and confetti and rice are symbols of the anticipated fertility of the marriage. Increasingly, as couples seek to create unique ceremonies that better suit their personal beliefs and lifestyles, some of these traditions are rejected, modified, or re-interpreted.

The celebrants we interviewed reported that most of their clients retain at least some wedding traditions, even though they do not always acknowledge the historical meanings behind them. For example, this young female celebrant commented:

> I'd say 80 percent of brides walk down the aisle with their dad. . . .
> Some of them have very big diamond rings, some of them don't . . .

but every bride has an engagement ring and then has a wedding ring and the guys always have wedding rings. . . . I suppose [the brides] all have bouquets and they still have their hair done. . . . They still walk down the aisle, so they still have that traditional element and they still get given away and they still do all of that. People think, oh this is how it's meant to be, so we'll do it like this. They buy *Bride and Groom* magazines and they go to wedding shows and . . . all of the dresses are white . . . . I suppose it's the whole cultural thing.

Somewhat surprisingly, the male ministers of religion were amused and sometimes angered by the retention of these symbols, talking about them as "patriarchal" or "sexist." For example, an older male minister who was also an independent celebrant, said:

When it comes to weddings . . . people are very, very traditional and find it very hard to break away from those sorts of traditional norms. . . . Even if we have a wedding in the garden, they'll talk about going down the *aisle*. . . . I think that women, in particular, have sort of fairy tale ideas about marriage, which is quite inappropriate. . . . I think they pick them out of popular culture.

The three male ministers of religion all reported that they tried to talk couples out of specific ceremonial practices, or at least encouraged them to reconsider the implications of including them. Another older male minister said:

The women always want a man to give them away, which I find quite abhorrent. I won't do the giving away thing because I think that's inappropriate in this day and age. . . . I think almost 99 percent of weddings the bride will be escorted in by her father. . . . That's okay to a degree, but I mean I won't ask a question of the father: "Who gives this woman away?" I won't do that because I think that's inappropriate because women aren't chattels to be passed around between the men folk.

The youngest minister in our study spoke of requests for new practices within wedding ceremonies that couples saw on television. He felt that some of these practices actually reflected old-fashioned ideas about gender relations and the nature of marriage:

> People watch things like weddings on *Shortland Street*.[3] So very occasionally couples turn up with ideas about things that they want to incorporate . . . such as the lighting of candles and having candle ceremonies. Often it's the bride and the groom who take the light from two candles and then light one candle and . . . they blow the other two out. . . . What is that saying about a relationship? It's saying that we're no longer individuals—there's just the marriage and nothing else. I don't like that symbolism, so I don't do that.

Celebrants also agreed that most couples are unaware of the original meanings behind wedding traditions, simply seeing them as the way weddings are done. As one female celebrant noted: "I don't think a woman who's about to get married and thinking what dress am I going to have, I don't think it even crosses her mind, 'Oh I'm not a virgin, I won't wear white'. It's a wedding dress. . . . I think it's the tradition of the colour rather than what it used to stand for."

The literature contains conflicting interpretations of the retention of patriarchal symbols and practices in many contemporary weddings. Currie (1993), for instance, notes that the appeal of the traditional wedding for women who seek egalitarian relationships lies in its transient nature; a conventional wedding is not necessarily a harbinger of things to come. Similarly, Otnes and Pleck (2003) argue that the patriarchal character of conventional weddings continues despite pressures for progressive change in women and men's lives. In contrast, Geller (2001: 70) claims that because "culture is cumulative" weddings are inevitably "tainted by the historical residue of female subordination."

---

3. *Shortland Street* is a New Zealand soap opera that runs on primetime television.

Many of the celebrants and heterosexual participants in our study described "modern traditional" weddings (Currie 1993: 404). These are weddings where many traditional aspects of the ceremony are retained such as walking the bride down the aisle, while other aspects are modified such as writing personalized vows. However, the symbolic meaning of the traditions that are retained, or the relevance to their own lives, is seldom questioned, even though other traditional aspects are rejected altogether. For example, few contemporary heterosexual brides promise in the ceremony to obey the groom, and this requirement has been removed from most wedding ceremonies. In our study, modern traditional weddings were more prevalent among the young different-sex couples entering marriage, while different-sex couples entering civil unions were more likely to opt for simpler affairs.

There was considerable variability in our study over which traditional elements were retained and which were not. Variations were also apparent in the degree to which any particular wedding could be called "traditional." For example, a young married mother around thirty talked about their wedding which was what she had always wanted:

> We had the classic big white dress wedding, not too gigantic, about seventy guests, ceremony was at [downtown church] and then the reception was at [x] restaurant. It was a pretty standard relatively expensive white wedding. . . . I had always wanted to get married in a big stone church when I was little. This church fitted the bill because of its very progressive viewpoints.

Another married woman in her late thirties talked about the importance of incorporating Christian traditions into their low-key wedding at a rented holiday cottage near the beach:

> We opted for a simple traditional Christian ceremony and I think that probably surprised some of our friends because we're not practising Christians as I said. But I did feel for me—I was raised

in kind of high church Anglican and my partner was raised a
Catholic so those rituals and things are part of how we see ourselves—even if it's not currently what we do. It's how we were
raised and what we grew up in and so that kind of environment is
certainly not alien and we hadn't strongly rejected it.

Likewise a married man around forty years old from a visible
minority background invoked the notion of tradition when he discussed their second wedding ceremony, which was held in a simple
bush camp and was not legally binding. The actual legal ceremony
had already taken place the day before at the registry office in town.
He described the non-legal ceremony:

It was formal, very formal. It had traditional elements of a
Western wedding in terms of [partner] walking down the aisle
with bridesmaids and I was waiting for her to come down the
aisle. That's very traditional, with the guests seated.

Participants entering civil unions also relied on some traditional wedding practices, despite the potential for creating a new kind
of ceremony or altering the symbolism. For example, a woman in
a different-sex civil union who was about thirty years old wore a
long conventional wedding dress. Another young woman who is
planning a different-sex civil union talked about the forthcoming
event this way:

It's still quite traditional. I mean I'm not wearing white but there's
still a dress, there's still flowers but the service doesn't reference
God or husband and wife. We're actually having our civil union
in an old church which is deconsecrated because it's now considered an historic building and the format is going to be pretty
straight forward . . . it's pretty traditional really.

Many of the same-sex civil unions were less conventional than
the heterosexual marriages, although both men and women usually

dressed up for the ceremony and hosted a meal and/or a party afterward. For example, two men in their fifties worked the morning of their wedding and then took the afternoon off to have a civil union in the registry office, dressed in their business suits. Later, one partner's daughter joined the couple and their sibling witnesses for champagne and afternoon tea in a nearby fancy hotel. A few weeks later, they hosted a party on a Sunday afternoon to celebrate their civil union, with forty to fifty guests, but exchanged their rings privately and unromantically after both events were over.

A young female couple in their twenties were still in the process of planning their wedding at the time of the interview but were not making much progress with differing ideas about the event. The older woman wanted a beach wedding with a traditional wedding dress and an overseas honeymoon, and admitted that she was influenced by the glamour of the recent royal wedding. The younger one, who talked about marriage as a "sensible lifestyle choice," would prefer a functional wedding with "no fuss," where she can wear shorts and a shirt, and later have a local honeymoon.

Another gay couple hosted an expensive event for a large number of guests in an out-of-town venue. This couple created a unique ceremony by blending traditions from each of their cultures. For example, the partner with strong ties to his European lineage spoke of starting their wedding in a traditional fashion "where the groom normally goes to the bride's house and knocks three times on the door and then he's let in to see the bride." Having deliberately stayed in separate rooms in the same hotel the night before, this participant went and knocked on his partner's door and was let in to see him for the first time that day.

In the past, weddings were typically seen as a sacrament before God, and they still are for religious people. Regular church attendees or those who come from religious families are still more likely than non-believers to choose marriage over cohabitation, to marry in a religious venue, and to expect a conventional family life (Dempsey and de Vaus 2004; Wu and Schimmele 2009). This is true of both different-sex and same-sex couples. However, few of our participants were married in churches or by religious celebrants. In fact, some of the different-sex couples who married in church or used ministers of religion as celebrants appeared to be seeking traditional weddings in picturesque settings or were attempting to please parents, rather than desiring a religious ceremony that required the blessing of God or the church congregation. Two of the ministers in our study expressed concern about what they saw as a trend toward secularism. One minister said:

> One of the big things is . . . because I've got a pretty church— I have pretty church syndrome—people want to come and get married here. . . . There are occasional requests: "Can we have our own celebrant?" We have a policy there that we don't have civil celebrants. We say, "If you're coming to a church, God's going to turn up at your wedding."

Another older minister lamented at length about the secularization of wedding ceremonies, even when they are held in church:

> I have always had what I call a marriage service kit and it has lots of choices and options . . . about seven different ways of introducing the service, a number of different prayers, a whole range of religious and non-religious readings, a range of vows or range of questions to the couple, vows and so on. . . . Within those choices people always have the option to take pieces from one bit and from another bit and marry them together so it's an endless infinite variety of possibilities. . . . Even the religious options are becoming more secular if you like. People will be less inclined to choose readings from the Bible for instance, and I've had to sort of think about that. Should I say "I think we should have one from the Bible?" But in the end I think, no this is their ceremony. Most of the people who I conduct weddings for turn up because [church's name] is a nice church, it's an attractive building. . . . So they're not necessarily church-attending people anyway.

These interview comments suggest that many couples want picturesque church weddings that retain some traditions but do not necessarily accept the view of marriage perpetuated by the clergy or church congregation. Increasingly, different-sex and same-sex couples expect celebrants, both independent and religious, to accommodate their secular ideas about how weddings should be performed, and want to craft their own particular blend of the traditional and modern wedding. Where do these ideas come from, how much do weddings cost, and what do they represent?

Weddings as Public Displays

Ideas about weddings are often garnered from other family members and past practices but they also come from childhood ideals, imagery from popular culture, aspects of celebrity events, or ideas from wedding exhibitions, magazines, or Internet sites. Research on heterosexual couples indicates that couples who decide to formalize their relationships expect to have saved enough money to afford a "real wedding," which typically means one that suitably commemorates this important event in their life and symbolically marks the transition to a new and more committed stage in their relationship (Cherlin 2004). Some couples also use their weddings to display their wealth or desired socio-economic status (Cherlin 2004; Sassler and Miller 2011).

The amount of money that people are willing to spend on weddings varies substantially by individual and couple, by who is paying the bills, by the couple's social class and cultural background, and by their stage in the family life cycle. The wedding industry encourages couples to spend lavishly on their weddings, and has "commodified" or offered as paid services, much of the wedding planning and preparation work traditionally done within families by brides and their mothers (Blakely 2008; Ingraham 2008; Otnes and Pleck 2003). The average cost of weddings was between $20,000 and $30,000 in Canada (Canadian Wedding Guide 2012) and over $25,600 (US) in the United States (Wedding Report 2012), and appears to be rising in many countries. As more couples are older when they marry and less reliant on parental financial support, the perceived cost and time involved in wedding preparations are additional reasons for young couples to postpone the event (Smock et al. 2005). However, studies find that weddings that are remarriages for at least one partner tend to be less elaborate and costly, suggesting that the first marriage is considered to be a more important rite of passage involving more planning and preparation (Humble 2009).

In our 2011 interviews, we asked both celebrants and cohabitants to estimate the amount of money that was spent on weddings, both those involving marriages and those involving civil unions. Some celebrants had no idea, but others suggested that couples typically paid from $10,000 to $50,000 (New Zealand) or more,[4] although some celebrants noted that they had also presided over lower-cost weddings. For example, a female celebrant talked about how expensive some same-sex civil unions can be when she said:

> I did a ceremony for a young lesbian couple last year and they both had full-on wedding dresses. It was at [a venue] on the waterfront. That would have set them back a fair bit. It was the full wedding, sit down, formal photos at [a regional park] before. Totally the wedding and I don't think they would have got much change out of [NZ] $25,000 probably.

A young recently married celebrant, in discussing wedding expenditures, mentioned the cost of her own different-sex wedding:

> I did my fiftieth wedding on the weekend and they hired out [X] Restaurant on a Saturday night. I can only imagine that would have been in the tens of thousands of dollars. I've done cheaper weddings where there're only a couple of people. I've done more expensive weddings. I'd say the average would be about as much as I spent on mine, which was about $30,000.

---

4.   The value of the NZ dollar was equivalent to about 85 cents Canadian at the time of the interviews.

For young couples, $30,000 represents a large proportion of their annual income and could require them to postpone the event or take out a loan, or to delay paying off other loans, buying a home, or starting a family.

Celebrants also reported that parents no longer pay the entire cost of weddings as many did in the past. Now, more couples pay for their own events because they are older, are employed, live independently from their parents, or, in the case of most same-sex couples, because their parents and family are ambivalent or even hostile about their weddings. An older male celebrant talked about prevalent practices:

> The couple would pay for the weddings themselves, whereas in years gone by it was the bride's parents who would pay for the wedding. Not nowadays. Most couples do the whole thing themselves, organize it themselves. Sometimes the brides' parents or mothers are involved . . . the parents might chip in but as I say, I don't think really that the parents pay for the whole thing.

The cohabitants were also asked about the total cost of their wedding or civil union, and their answers ranged from less than $500 to $35,000 (New Zealand). Some couples spent considerable amounts of money, despite having few assets, living on a low income, or in some cases being in debt. For example, a young married woman described her heterosexual wedding, which cost over $30,000, as:

> Kind of full-on. Just what you would want as a woman getting married, I guess. Like, we got married at [x] vineyard. We kind of made a weekend of it. We had about ninety family and friends there. It was just perfect really. Just everything I wanted. Very traditional. . . . We wrote our own vows and just a big party kind of thing afterwards.

One reason why weddings cost so much money is that wedding planners, celebrants, and venue owners all need to be paid a fee. Another reason for expensive weddings is that more couples are choosing to combine a wedding with a holiday or honeymoon in an exotic destination. "Wedding tourism" contributes considerable funds to local economies and for this reason is often promoted by governments as well as private entrepreneurs who own vineyards, hotels, and resorts. Countries such as New Zealand have become destinations for overseas couples to legalize their relationships (Husbands 2006; Johnston 2006), and particularly attracts same-sex couples entering civil unions as they are not always legally available in the couple's country of residence (Baker and Elizabeth 2012c). As we noted in Chapter 1, about 10 percent of marriages and nearly 19 percent of civil unions taking place in New Zealand were registered to overseas residents in 2009, and many of these couples travelled from jurisdictions in Australia and the United States where the possibility for the legalization of same-sex relationships is limited (Statistics New Zealand 2010c). Weddings clearly provide a significant source of revenue for entrepreneurs and governments, but they also provide relationship rights and memorable celebratory events for couples and their friends and families.

A few couples in our study talked about their "destination weddings" that were combined with a honeymoon. For example, a young female student in a different-sex relationship discussed her overseas beach wedding in which she wore a long white dress and veil, her father walked her "down the aisle" (along the sand), and they were married by a local minister:

> It was a traditional wedding. It was quite small because people had to fly into [name of Pacific island]. There were thirty-eight people and it was on the beach . . . they had a sort of large thatched hut that was open to the sea and we had like a barbecue buffet where they were cooking the food. Then like a dance floor area and stuff there as well and we had our kind of top table thing across one side so looking out to the water. . . . We actually went to [another

Pacific island] for our honeymoon so that was really cool. So two days after the wedding we flew over there for five nights. . . . The resort was really good. . . . If you stayed there a certain amount of nights you got the wedding package for free and all these kind of cool things that they did.

Although the amount of money spent by the couple on this overseas wedding was surprisingly low, the cost was presumably higher than normal for the guests.

A few participants in our interviews said they wanted relatively modest and non-traditional weddings, and married in the cheapest possible way for pragmatic reasons. For example, an older woman who married over a decade ago to enable her long-term male partner to live with her in another country clearly thought traditional weddings were a waste of money:

Proper weddings kind of seem middle class to me. . . . Oh they're expensive for a start. It seems like a bad value way to spend money to me. Especially if you see young couples where they haven't got any property and they haven't got much stuff and there's talk of a wedding costing $8,000 or something and you think why don't you just give them the money and let them get a sort of grounding?

A lesbian who married her partner of many years talked of wanting to elope so they could have the smallest ceremony possible. However, her partner wanted to have a public ceremony and "the whole shebang." What this couple came up with was an intimate ceremony with about twenty family and friends followed by a self-catered party at a friend's house for just over seventy guests. Nevertheless the wedding still cost them about $5,000, a sum that she found shocking:

It was a hell of a lot more than we wanted to spend. I didn't want to spend, I wanted to spend the minimum amount of money that we could on it. . . . In fact when it all added up I was just mortified and shocked that we could possibly have spent $5,000, but at the same time we wanted to provide the food and we wanted to be the hosts.

Another man in his thirties, who had a civil union in the garden of his female partner's parents, talked about trying to keep the expenses down when he said:

We'd had some friends who had got married a year earlier who spent about forty grand. . . . It was really lovely, it was a really nice wedding but we just kind of find that absolutely abominably ridiculous and so we were really determined to do things on the cheap so we kind of decided that we wouldn't spend more than like two or three hundred bucks on buying stuff for ourselves to wear so, yeah, [partner] kind of found something that was incredibly flash but really, really cheap. What I was wearing and the hat that I was wearing it was kind of like, hey this will work.

A man is his late thirties, who was planning a same-sex civil union, talked about his distaste for expensive weddings:

Well one of the reasons we didn't want a traditional wedding was we didn't want to blow $30,000 on one day, because I think it's a little bit silly. But certainly when we originally started planning it, because we thought we would go to [x] Island and book a house, two houses out for three or four days, it ended up it was going to be about that sort of money. So we're quite keen not to just spend a whole lot of money on one day. So hence why we thought we would have the ceremony at home and we would go around to a friend's place for a reception/party and that would cut out all the venue costs.

Many couples had what we have called do-it-yourself (DIY) weddings. Such weddings were usually held in family members' gardens or in other modest venues such as holiday homes and community halls. Most involved significant contributions by the couple and their family and friends in the production of the event, and in many cases, the contributions took the form of gifts. As one recently married female participant explained:

> A workmate of mine made the wedding cake . . . and people from work contributed towards that, so that was their gift to us, which was really lovely. And my aunty made my wedding dress, so that was her gift. A friend, a couple of people did food, and that was their gift. They did a lot of food, so it was really nice.

DIY weddings were largely motivated by budgetary constraints, which men in different-sex relationships seemed more concerned about. For instance, one recently married man in his late twenties spoke of his determination to gain a material advantage from his "investment" in a wedding ceremony, which was held in the backyard of their home:

> The type of wedding we had with me deciding that we were going to do it in the backyard or not at all sort of thing, and people look at that like a cost saving measure, but basically I just thought to myself that if we were going to spend $10,000 or $12,000 having a party or something, you know like a celebration day for a wedding, that I was going to get something out of it permanent. So I decided to invest a bit of money on the house, build a new deck, put a fence up, sort of clean the place up.

Most women in our study, especially those in different-sex relationships, willingly went along with the budgetary constraints of the DIY wedding. However, they often made budgetary exceptions for their wedding dresses because, as one woman said: "You have to wear a nice frock for it to be a wedding." Sometimes the budgetary exception took the form of buying expensive material from which a friend or relative would create the all-important dress. One woman with an insecure job, a child, and a mortgage had a very modest wedding with her family and friends and told us that her wedding dress was made by a friend for free. However, it included several lengths of fabric costing $300 per metre, which meant she "did have to spend a bit of money on it, not thousands but hundreds." This dress was not white and could be adapted for later use but it was full length and had a train, even though the wedding was held in an inexpensive community hall in the bush.

Others were enchanted by the possibility of named designer dresses, despite having unconventional ideas about marriage and a limited income. For instance one woman in a different-sex civil union said:

> This is the bit where I sound really, really conventional. I actually had a kind of pale cream long dress. I came across this dress in the Myer[5] design department and it was reduced, it was like this amazing [named designer] dress . . . . And it happened to be reduced from three and a half thousand dollars to $150 and it was like neat. So I kind of wore a weddingy kind of dress.

The willingness to make an exception for the wedding dress can be in part explained by the dreams that girls and young women have about their weddings, dreams which typically centre on their wedding dresses. For example, a mother in her late thirties, who had cohabited for ten years before marrying, talked about her wedding dress:

> I didn't actually want to spend a lot of fussing over a dress, which sounds odd because I do love fashion and I do think that the dress is a really vital part of my enjoyment of the day. So I talked to my friends about it. . . . I had in the back of my mind when I was young I had imagined a wedding dress that was a bit more

---

5.   Myer is an Australian department store.

1920s than it was full length and all that kind of stuff and I just kept an eye out and oddly enough one weekend in the Canvas magazine there was this great [designer] dress that was styled in quite a 1940s way and I looked at it and thought I could wear this for my wedding. . . . I wanted to get it in a lovely blue colour, but they only had ivory. But it was beautiful and it was a very rich ivory, creamy colour that I felt was okay for a more aged bride than white. . . . My partner found . . . something in the window of [designer clothing store] and thought that would be great and went in and tried it on and it was perfect. So he got a great suit and I got a great dress.

As these comments about wedding clothes suggest, the cost of weddings varied considerably among our participants, showing that not everyone is equally influenced by social pressure to consume or engage in "conspicuous consumption." Couples of a more mature age and those who were marrying for the second time tended to opt for minimal weddings that cost very little. In comparison, most of those who had expensive and lavish weddings were different-sex couples aged in their late twenties to early forties, who were marrying for the first time. Perhaps their willingness to spend large sums of money on their wedding relates to the fact that the first marriage is considered a more significant rite of passage than subsequent unions, and because younger people are more vulnerable to social pressure about what constitutes a "proper" wedding.

Generally speaking, younger same-sex and different-sex women seemed more inclined than men to spend money on their weddings, and most different-sex women reported they were willing to stretch their wedding budgets to gain a memorable wedding dress. Only one heterosexual woman in our study reported that she had hired her wedding dress as part of a deliberate strategy to minimize the costs of their wedding, which still ended up being over $15,000. But different-sex couples who entered civil unions tended to spend less than the married couples as they were more likely to hold unconventional attitudes about marriage, money, and gender roles.

Like their different-sex counterparts, the wedding expenditure of same-sex couples varied considerably, but the most expensive wedding in our interviews was reported by two gay men.

Conclusions

Clearly, decisions to formalize relationships and the ceremonies and celebrations chosen for weddings are influenced by many factors. These include personal values, the age of the couple, their sexual orientation, and the financial resources available to them, but marriage decisions are also shaped by social pressures, images from the media, and the wedding industry. Decisions are often negotiated between couples where the importance of having a public celebration is not always shared equally by each partner. In our interviews, the women in heterosexual relationships were more likely than the men to expect to plan and host a memorable "event," to spend money to achieve their aspirations for this event, and to enjoy the personal attention they received from friends and family over their wedding. Some participants, especially men, seemed embarrassed by the fuss, attention, and high cost of the weddings planned by their partners. For example, one man in his late twenties, whose wife had urged him to marry, said that he would have preferred to go to the registry office but his partner wanted a big wedding with seventy or more guests. He insisted on marrying in the back garden of their house or not at all, and spent some of the wedding money on improvements to the yard, which helped him to justify the expense.

The widespread trend for couples to pay for much of their own wedding helps explain why so many postpone the event until they can save enough money for a "real" wedding but also why weddings have become increasingly personalized and elaborate. Older and financially independent couples command a stronger negotiating position with their respective families about the nature of their wedding, yet many of the older couples in our study opted for simpler and less expensive events.

The research discussed in this chapter suggests that many couples continue to rely on age-old wedding traditions, some of which have been associated with patriarchy and heterosexism, without acknowledging or dwelling on their symbolic meaning. When planning their weddings, both men and women, and those in different-sex and same-sex relationships, draw on their early gender socialization, their cultural traditions, other weddings they have attended, and current trends from popular culture. Celebrants and wedding organizers may contribute suggestions but magazines and celebrity weddings help to shape prevalent ideas about how these events can be or should be performed. The wedding "industry" spends billions of dollars producing exhibitions, magazines and fashion items, and these particularly influence younger women when they plan their "big day."

In the next chapter, we examine the personalization of weddings, including not only the kinds of modifications that are made but also the kinds of couples who are likely to make major changes to traditional wedding practices. Both our interviews and the previous research concludes that many couples see their weddings as opportunities to show their creativity and innovation, to "create their own personal biography," and to have an informal but celebratory party with family and friends. However, a few of our participants wanted a memorable and extravagant event that made them feel like a wealthy celebrity for the day.

CHAPTER 4

Personalized Weddings

Introduction

Previous research suggests that many cohabiting couples who eventually marry expect to personalize their wedding ceremonies and celebrations to reflect their values and lifestyles. In her history of American wedding culture, Carol Wallace (2004) argues that the shift toward unique and personalized weddings began in the 1970s, a process that accelerated in the 1990s according to Husbands (2006). Wallace claims that personalized weddings emerged against a backdrop of the sustained critique of marriage by the women's movement and other counter-cultural movements of the 1960s and 1970s. By personalizing their weddings, couples believed they were not dupes of social convention, but rather the creators of their own destinies. The notion that a couple's wedding ceremony and marriage could be personally crafted to suit their own tastes and values also chimed with the rhetoric of the New Right, a pro-market political force that became increasingly influential across the English-speaking world from the late 1970s onward, and which emphasized the liberal values of personal choice and freedom.

Yet, as Husbands' (2006) analysis of nearly twenty years of wedding magazines in New Zealand shows, the shift to personalized weddings has not been accompanied by the wholesale rejection of wedding practices that we have come to regard as "traditional" (for example, the wearing of a long white wedding dress or the swapping of wedding rings, both of which are relatively recent additions to the conventional wedding). On the contrary, Husbands details the way that wedding magazines encourage couples, and especially brides, to express their individuality through a seemingly unique combination of new and traditional elements in their wedding

ceremonies. In retaining at least some traditional wedding practices, Husbands suggests that wedding couples selectively tap into
the meanings of these traditions. Stripped of their usually patriarchal meanings, wedding traditions instead stand in for a link with
a mythical past that was characterized by the stability and permanence of marital bonds.

The idea that weddings can and should be personally tailored
events has received renewed emphasis with the legalization and
rise to social prominence of same-sex weddings or their equivalent. Given the historical absence of rituals that publicly recognize
and celebrate same-sex relationships, gay and lesbian couples who
marry face a dilemma and a choice: should they emulate the conventions of the heterosexual wedding ritual, in part or in whole, or
should they create a new tradition? Research into same-sex wedding ceremonies suggests that the responses of same-sex couples
to this dilemma is informed by their political sensibilities and lies
along a continuum from the straight and conventional to the exotic
and flamboyantly queer (Smart 2008).

In this chapter, we investigate the expectations that our participants had for personalized weddings, as we consider the role of
professional celebrants, websites, television programs, magazines,
and particularly friends in promoting ideas about unique and personal weddings. The chapter will also explore some of the changing
ways of conducting wedding ceremonies and celebrations, and the
actual practices of the participants we interviewed in New Zealand.
We also examine what difference it makes to the type of ceremony
if couples are entering a marriage or a civil union, if they are older
or younger, are parents or not, or are part of a same-sex or different-sex couple. The basic question asked in this chapter is, what
do current wedding practices reveal about people's aspirations and
lifestyles, and the kind of society in which we now live?

We noted in Chapter 1 that some jurisdictions continue to permit only members of the clergy and certain municipal government
officials to marry couples. However, those jurisdictions which have
expanded the range of marriage celebrants who are independent of

the church or state have witnessed a rise in personalized weddings. In our New Zealand–based study, the ten celebrants we interviewed all suggested that standardized weddings are now a thing of the past and the interviews with cohabitants further illustrated the personalization of weddings, including unique marriage proposals, memorable venues, reconfigured vows, unusual poems and music, non-traditional outfits, and receptions or parties in special places.

As we outlined in Chapter 2, participants in our study told us about stage-managed proposals in helicopters and on mountain tops, and more casual ones by email or on the living room couch, proposals made after family crises, and particularly those made while on holiday. Couples married or had their civil unions on cliff-tops and beaches, in public parks and private gardens, in de-consecrated and functioning churches, in registry offices, and especially in commercial wedding venues. Their ceremonies included readings from different cultures, eras, and religions, and poems, videos, musical performances, and speeches delivered by relatives, friends, and their children as well as by their celebrant. Although couples were often uncertain about which aspects of the ceremony they could alter, they almost invariably expected them to be a unique blend of traditional and newer elements that reflected their personal beliefs, circumstances, and aspirations. This has also been found in the wider research (Boden 2003; Currie 1993; Otnes and Pleck 2003).

Weddings have become more unique and elaborate events because of the introduction of independent celebrants, the rise of consumerism and individualism, pressure from the wedding industry, and the trend for couples to marry when they are older and therefore to pay for their own wedding. A young minister in our study reinforced the idea that paying for one's own wedding augments the possibilities of personalization and higher expenditure when he said:

> Young professional couples tend to put money into their wedding
> in a way that didn't use to happen, whereas it used to be that the

parents of the bride just copped the bill for the lot. There's still a degree of that but it's far more of a, well: "We're putting money into this and this is what we want." So most couples have a stronger ground to negotiate with their respective families about what it is they want.

Our combined research suggests that what couples want to include in their wedding seems to be influenced by a number of factors, including what their friends suggest or have already done in their weddings and advice from parents, siblings, wedding magazines, and independent celebrants. Many of our participants told us that their marriage and civil union celebrants not only married them but also helped them to plan aspects of their wedding by suggesting certain practices, which we discuss in the next section.

Celebrants and Personalized Weddings

The cohabitants in our study sometimes selected celebrants who maximized their opportunities to create unique and personal ceremonies. For example, a young man who seemed to see himself as unconventional and inclusive mentioned that he and his female partner chose a gay celebrant to preside over their different-sex civil union and spoke of him in the following manner:

> He's a really neat guy and I think, he's laid back and we're laid back, and it will just make the wedding all kind of laid back and nice and relaxing. . . . He's got this awesome English accent. . . . And he's not overbearing. He's not hoity toity. He's not big into tradition for tradition's sake. He's really genuine.

A married woman about forty years old spoke with similar enthusiasm about their celebrant:

> She was amazing. We must have met with her two or three times for about three hours at a go and she could just see who we were and she picked out those bits from our conversation and put

together something that was us. Took our personalities and wove that together. So that was really magical. She was saying it's all about the ceremony, so the ceremony had to be really original, really original, and something with our mark on it.

In addition, some same-sex participants deliberately sought out a celebrant who shared their sexual preference. For example, a lesbian woman in her mid-twenties mentioned the importance of shared understandings when creating an individualized ceremony: "I worry whether a celebrant who is not queer actually understands the struggles and what it represents."

Most of the secular celebrants in our study believed couples came to them because they wanted a unique and personally crafted ceremony and they saw it as part of their duty to deliver ceremonies that reflected the couples with whom they were working. As one celebrant said:

> People are looking for ceremonies that have meaning for them, personal meaning, not something that maybe their parents might have had or grandparents. They still want it to be legal and meaningful but they really want to personalize it and make it what they want it to be.

Another celebrant in her fifties, who presides only over same-sex civil unions, embraced the trend toward personalization more than most when she said: "I perceive my job as to be providing the framework that allows them to have whatever they want and yeah I pretty much do just about anything really." She went on to say:

> I've got couple who are going to be on the beach. . . . They're talking jandals and casual gear but they still want the formal structure of the ceremony but in an informal situation, no religious stuff or anything like that. It's interesting because most people want to make a statement about their feelings and what they are

promising. . . . It's great and people are so diverse and so creative with it.

As a consequence, the celebrants prided themselves on offering an authentic and creative wedding ceremony, and some provided extensive premarital discussions and even counselling with clients. Some of the celebrants achieved this by keeping files of material on hand from which they could "cut and paste" and then added new items to suit each new pair of clients, while others insisted that they painstakingly create every wedding ceremony "from scratch." Particularly the women who were full-time secular celebrants took pleasure in tailoring ceremonies to their clients' wishes, as long as they met the minimal legal requirements. One such celebrant spoke of the lengths she went to "co-create" the wedding ceremony with couples:

> A lot of couples have a lot of ideas in their minds and don't know they've got the ideas and it's a question of just drawing them out. . . . So the co-creation is more about words that people are using. I ask all sorts of questions. It's a two hour interview . . . so that you've got their phrases that you then write back into the ceremony, and then the way I work is at the second meeting, which is again another two hour meeting . . . reading the ceremony to them . . . and when you watch them, hearing their own words back again. That's when you watch them just melt, that's when they fall in love with the ceremony.

Other celebrants were more measured and kept their meetings with their clients to a minimum because the creation of personalized weddings could easily become too time-consuming, considering their professional fee, which ranged from $250 to $1,000 (New Zealand; about $200 to $820 Canadian). However, the cohabitants sometimes rejected celebrants who attempted to modify their preliminary plans. For example, one young man who was about to have a different-sex civil union described the quest for the right celebrant in following way: "We just wanted to find someone who meshed with us and could understand us as a couple and not be too old-fashioned and uptight and would want us to have a ceremony however we want to have it." Clearly, creating individualized ceremonies is time-consuming, sometimes involving months of planning for the couples and numerous discussions with celebrants.

We interviewed four ministers of religion in our study, although only two had their own church. The church-based ministers talked the most about the trend toward personalized and secular weddings but also admitted that the couples they united were probably more traditional than those of secular celebrants. The church-based ministers clearly disapproved of requests to be married in their own church by a secular celebrant rather than themselves, and complained about couples who wanted to omit Bible readings and God from the ceremony. However, they mentioned that their churches provided some opportunity for couples to negotiate over particular words or phrases, even though couples were expected to choose one of the church's optional ceremonies that usually ranged from traditional to contemporary.

While the oldest minister, who was in his sixties, seemed to resent the secularization of weddings, the youngest one (in his thirties) saw himself as more flexible than most. He discussed at some length the continual requests he receives to secularize church weddings, including to bring in a secular celebrant to preside over the ceremony:

> Some Anglican ministers would insist upon there being a Bible reading—I don't. I think that readings are really one of those places where a couple can really have something that really expresses who they are and part of their identity. I've had it all—in terms of readings—from Shakespeare to Harry Potter. . . . Kahlil Gibran's reading from *The Prophet*. . . . I am happy to use it. So, it comes from a different faith tradition but it still says profound things about love and marriage, and why not?

These comments suggest that marrying couples are placing greater pressure on ministers and churches, as well as on independent celebrants, to modify their wedding practices.

Only a small minority of New Zealanders now marry in church. The oldest minister in our study talked about the changes in weddings over the years, including the trend toward secular weddings outside of churches:

> When I began in the ministry [thirty-seven years ago], you could only either get married by a church minister or in a registry office and I conducted quite a lot of weddings of people who didn't really identify as Christian but wanted something better than a registry office wedding. The number of weddings I preside over has decreased as weddings have become more popular with secular celebrants rather than in churches. . . . When I started, I remember one year in a country parish I had at least one wedding a weekend between Labour Weekend [October] one year and Easter [April] the next. Now in an urban parish and in a much different environment we would get about twelve weddings a year . . .

Creating personalized weddings as social events can also be sites of competition. As one independent celebrant observed:

> I think there's an unspoken social pressure and that couples can compete in some way for when they're getting engaged and when they're getting married and what they had at their ceremony. . . . Like one [wedding] I did on Friday night, the groom was talking to his mates while we were waiting for the bride and he said: "We've got the best celebrant, we've got the best photographer, we've done it at the best venue." You know, it's a bit competitive . . . who's got the biggest ring. . . .

This comment reflects the findings in the wider research that weddings continue to provide opportunities for couples and families to display their creativity to friends and family, as well as their social status or wealth. The next section examines the extent of personalization in the ceremonies of the participants in our study.

Details of Wedding Personalization

Most cohabitants in our study reported that they had personalized at least some aspects of their weddings. One woman in a same-sex relationship spoke fondly of their wedding invitations: "The invitations were very beautiful. . . . I'd been arrested many, many times for political action and so our civil union invitation said: 'From civil disobedience to civil union'. It was quite sweet." Most participants reported that they had written their own vows, although a few accepted the standard vows provided by the celebrant or registry office. For example, a gay man in his late fifties who had been living with his male partner for over twenty years laughed about their "functional" civil union at the registry office with two siblings as witnesses. He reported that the male registrar seemed to assume that they would have brought personalized vows with them:

> The celebrant said: "Have you prepared vows?" And we both looked blankly at each other, and I said: "No, we haven't thought about that." I said: "I'm sure you've got something on hand, something bog standard, just reel that out." It's not to diminish the vow or sense of the occasion at all. . . . So we read whatever the words were on a piece of paper.

Both men wanted to legalize their long-term relationship to ensure they would be treated as next of kin should one or the other become ill or die, but the subsequent celebratory party with friends seemed more significant when both individually recounted their wedding details in separate interviews.

The kind of wedding people desire tends to be influenced by their personal values, social and economic circumstances, and reasons for formalizing their relationship, but the details sometimes involved negotiations between couples or with parents. Our participants typically spoke of modifications to many aspects of weddings, such as changing the wording of the vows or the sex of attendants, adding the couple's favourite music or poems, wearing non-traditional outfits, buying unusual rings or presenting them in unique ways, or having both parents, mothers, or no one "give away" the bride.

After the wedding ceremony, most couples and their families offer food and drink to their guests, and speeches are typically made about the couple and their relationship. Many weddings also have a wedding cake, which is ceremonially cut by the couple while they are photographed. However, all these aspects of the wedding are open to personalization, but especially the venue, the colour scheme, the table decorations, and speeches. For example, a young woman in a different-sex relationship talked about their wedding reception, which was held in a rustic lodge near the sea after they married on the beach:

> We had these funny little Mexican skeletons for on top of the wedding cake. My friend had been to Mexico and I've always loved skeletons, so she brought me the bride when we got engaged because she was over there. . . . Also I really love vintage stuff so we hired Crown Lynn[1] swans for the tables, like little Crown Lynn swans that had flowers in them.

Regardless of the couple's sexual preference and whether they had a marriage or civil union, the weddings of most of our participants were personalized in some way. However, certain aspects were modified more often than others, such as unusual rings given in unusual places, wearing non-traditional outfits, expressing their feelings for each other during the wedding ceremony, and resisting patriarchal or inequitable vows. These are all discussed in the next section.

---

1.   Crown Lynn is a type of dinnerware popular in New Zealand in the 1950s, now a collector's item.

Unusual Rings Given in Unusual Places

Many participants mentioned their engagement or wedding rings in the interview, often as part of their proposal stories, and several told us that they bought their own engagement ring for various reasons. For example, a lesbian woman in her late twenties told the interviewer that she and her partner had mutually decided to have a civil union but this decision had received a poor reception from her parents and was therefore not publicly announced. Furthermore, she had always expected a traditional marriage proposal before her engagement was official:

> I had always wanted . . . to be like *properly* proposed to, like *properly*. So we didn't tell anybody that we were engaged, we just kept it to ourselves. I actually bought my own engagement ring while she was in South America and I just said: "You can propose whenever you're ready." Then one day she proposed. She did the whole romantic dinner . . . you know that kind of stuff and proposed to me [at the top of the local volcano]. So that was quite cool.

Several women who were trying to persuade their male partner to marry also bought their own ring, which sometimes led to a marriage proposal. For example, we already mentioned the woman over sixty years old who talked about buying an artisan jeweller's ring for herself while on holiday, after thirteen years of cohabitation, but to her surprise her partner offered to pay for it and then casually proposed an hour later. Another woman in her fifties, who has been cohabiting for over twelve years and decided to buy a dress ring, told us that her male partner redirected her attention to the engagement ring section of the jewellery store and instead bought her an engagement ring. However, he called it a "commitment ring" and did *not* propose marriage, which he apparently saw as unnecessary. Nevertheless, the woman reported that she was "engaged" and volunteered to be interviewed for our study. Others used "engagement" rings to stave off opposition from parents to their cohabitation. For example, a woman in her sixties reported that she and her male partner cohabited for nineteen years before marriage but after five years of cohabitation they had engagement rings made, partly as a joke but also to stifle any parental objections to their cohabitation.

Engagement rings were also hidden in strange places rather than presented directly to the partner. For example, a woman around thirty told a long story of her male partner hiding the engagement ring in a muffin while they were on a trip. Without telling her, he separately told both of her divorced parents that he was going to propose to her and then organized a weekend holiday for the two of them several hundred miles from home. During the drive there, he stopped at a bakery and bought sandwiches for lunch but also a chocolate muffin that was not eaten right away. When it was still sitting in the car the next day, she suggested that they should throw it away because it was stale, but he refused. That night they went to the theatre and afterward he suggested a walk in the park by the sea. She reported the events that followed:

> I sort of thought I don't really want to do that, it's a bit cold, I'm not really interested and he said: "No, come on, we'll go." So we went down and . . . walked around a bit and then he said: "Are you hungry?" and I said: "No, I've kind of just had dinner." And he said: "Why don't you have some of that chocolate muffin?" And I was like: "That chocolate muffin! I'm not trying that chocolate muffin, it's a day old!" But he managed to convince me to have some of this and he'd put the ring inside the chocolate muffin and it was only afterwards that I said: "Do you realize how many times I almost threw that muffin into the rubbish?" And so, I found the ring and he asked me to marry him.

In addition to hiding engagement rings in unusual places, the interviews revealed stories about wedding rings that demonstrate how weddings can be personalized. For example, a couple in their sixties had arranged for matching wedding rings to be made but they were not ready in time for the wedding, so they used two-dollar shell rings for the ceremony. A married man around forty talked about their unique wedding rings: "Both [partner's] and my wedding ring had our finger prints and [son's] toe prints on them as well. So [son's] toe prints are on the middle and [partner's] and my fingerprints are on the outside." A gay man in his late fifties spoke of their matching wedding rings, although his was given to him by his male partner for his birthday, well before they decided to have a civil union. A woman in her mid-thirties talked about her two weddings—one that was legal and one that was "real." The second (but non-legal) wedding involved a Buddhist ceremony modified slightly by a Presbyterian celebrant, where they passed the wedding rings around and asked guests to bless them while her male partner's friend played the double bass. These examples all show the various ways that participants retained the traditional symbolism of the engagement ring or wedding ring, while adding their personal touches.

Several of the same-sex couples spoke about their use of other symbols of unity and permanence, either as part of the ceremony itself or a lasting marker of their changed status. For example, a woman in a same-sex civil union described her partner's use of stones during the ceremony to create an infinity symbol in the form of a figure eight, which she and their guests found very meaningful. Two gay men took the rather unusual step of having matching tattoos on their forearms in the lead-up to the wedding which one of them likened to a "diamond ring":

> This is my first tā moko (tattoo) that I've ever had and for me the experience of having this tā moko wasn't about putting ink on my skin, it was about releasing something that's been lying there waiting to be seen. That's the experience. . . . And I feel to be honest when I go like that it feels like a diamond ring to me. It's a very powerful feeling to have this on here and that's once again another symbol that reinforces the relationship we have and the love we have.

In addition, participants talked about what they wore to their wedding, which is discussed in the next section.

Wearing Non-Traditional Outfits

Many women in our study reported that they wore traditional white/ivory dresses while men often reported wearing formal or dark suits to their wedding but some participants mentioned that they or their partners wore non-traditional outfits. For example, a woman in a same-sex civil union talked about the outfits they wore to their wedding, which was held in a park overlooking the Pacific Ocean: "I wore a red dress, just really simple red dress. We decided to have colours of black, red, white and silver and [partner] wore black and I wore red. . . . They were really similar dresses but hers was just a little bit different cut to mine." However, her partner, who we interviewed separately, talked about initially wanting to wear white but "then [partner's] mother had a bit of an issue with it and she said: 'Oh that will make it look like you're the bride and she's not.' . . . So I went: 'Oh okay, I will actually wear black because I like black.'"

Several women in different-sex relationships also spoke of choosing non-traditional styles and colours for wedding dresses that were specifically made for the occasion by family members or friends. This was often because they wanted to remodel their dresses so they could wear them later, as this brief snippet from a recently married young woman makes clear: "I wore a bright vivid purple dress instead of the traditional white or cream or ivory. So I can wear it again which I did. I'm very happy about that." Another woman in her forties who was married recently in a burgundy-coloured dress also emphasized the utilitarian motive that lay behind her choice of her wedding dress:

One of the bridesmaids made my dress for me, which was not a traditional wedding dress at all. . . . . We came up with a design that I knew would work for me and it was a skirt and top. It was a very long skirt but she chopped it off afterwards so that I could wear it again and the top wasn't a particularly wedding top so I've worn that quite a bit as well.

Another woman, who had previously discussed her non-traditional different-sex civil union, guiltily reported that she wore a long cream wedding dress made by a renowned designer, which she had purchased because of its cut-down price. However, she quickly added that her male partner wore a less traditional "wedding" outfit: "He wore some khaki trousers and an untucked shirt, no tie, and a panama hat. I think he took the hat off during the ceremony." A woman in her sixties, who had married largely to obtain a visa for her long-term male partner before they lived overseas, talked about her functional wedding in the registry office:

> I did wear clothes I thought were attractive. . . . I bought some expensive tights that were patterned. I wore my boots which were fairly stompish and I think I had a nice silk skirt. But they were clothes I wore all the time. I just chose things that I thought would be quite nice. Then that night we took [the witness and partner] out for dinner. . . . But the whole thing was sort of tongue in cheek.

While most of the same-sex couples in our study did not engage in what Smart (2008) called demonstrative weddings that contained flamboyant displays of homosexuality, one couple nevertheless decided to explicitly code their wedding as a gay event through the use of black and pink as their theme colours:

> We realized that apart from the fact that we're both males, we weren't really gaying the wedding up very much. And the first thing we thought was to get a friend who does drag shows to be a drag performer, maybe when we were signing the register, could do a drag show out the front. And then we thought even better we can make a theme of black and pink, we will wear black and

pink and we want our invitations to be black and pink and we would like everyone who's coming to be fabulous in black and pink. And a few people actually said: "That's kind of gay isn't it? Isn't that a little too gay?." . . . We thought well actually that makes us more want to make it black and pink.

Despite such minor departures, few of the cohabiting participants reported that they wore *very* unusual outfits to their weddings. However, the celebrants told us stories of some of their clients who openly flaunted wedding traditions in this respect. For example, a celebrant talked about a ceremony she recently presided over:

They'd both be about twenty-three but they've got heaps of bridesmaids. He's got four groomsmen and she's got three bridesmaids and two *bridesmen* because she's got two best friends who are blokes, and so five of those are going to walk ahead of her and they're all wearing black. The bride isn't but you find a lot of bridesmaids these days are wearing quite whacky colours, like black.

Occasionally cohabitants in our study spoke about non-traditional clothing for their attendants. A young heterosexual couple, who chose civil union rather than marriage, also chose a non-traditional configuration for their "bridesmaids" and "groomsmen":

We're just wearing suits. . . . I've got two female groomsmen and the decision to put them into suits as well was interesting. But to be honest they both really look good in suits. . . . We did have to think because one of [my partner's] bridesmaids is a guy as well. But we're not putting him in a dress or anything, I don't believe. But it just worked with the groom's side all being in suits and the girls look great in it, so yeah we're just going for that.

Another celebrant talked about her clients, particularly one couple in a same-sex civil union who dressed like heterosexual couples:

I've done a large number of same-sex women, lesbian women, and very often one of them will dress in a feminine outfit and the other one will dress in a masculine outfit. It's really quite strange. In fact I did one just last week and that's exactly what happened. They were an Asian couple, Chinese couple and one of them wore, I mean black trousers and a black jacket and a bow tie, essentially it was a very feminine looking suit but it was a suit and the other wore this lovely red, nice red short dress and I mean it was very feminine so one was very feminine and the other one was quite masculine.

A middle-aged lesbian woman who had recently entered a civil union with her long-term partner drew on the rather stereotypical idea that same-sex weddings involve mimicry of "hetero-gendered" clothing to tease her mother about the format of her own civil union. She said:

When I rang my mother and said we were going to have a civil union, she asked: "What are you going to do about clothes?" And I said: "Well I'm going to wear a frilly white top and [partner] is going to wear a tux top and a white skirt and I'm going to wear a frilly white top and black trousers and half way through the ceremony we're going to swap so we're going to go as half the bride and half the groom and then we're going to swap over." Well my poor mother she didn't know what to believe or what to think. And I said: "No mum it's alright, we're not doing any of that stuff. It's not a wedding, you don't have to worry, you don't have to bring presents, there's no wedding, no name change and we won't be wearing gowns and tuxedos."

Although they didn't wear traditional wedding attire, this couple each bought "fabulous outfits" that that were out of ordinary for them and consisted of "groovy" skirts and tops.

A third celebrant talked about a same-sex civil union where everyone wore jeans and T-shirts:

I do recall one ceremony that I attended. . . . This [lesbian] couple were so informal . . . they hired some place down on the Auckland Viaduct that looked out onto the water. It must have cost a fortune and . . . they basically had said that the dress code was jeans and T-shirts, you know very casual. That's what they turned up in and they stood around and started drinking and I had to stop them before they got too trashed.

This same celebrant reported another same-sex civil union where the male couple flaunted traditional dress codes:

I have seen a DVD of a ceremony where the service was conducted by a drag queen in full drag and the person is a celebrant. . . . Many of the guests were in full drag and that was what they liked. That was part of their community and friends, so it was completely appropriate for them.

The celebrants typically reported that gay men are most likely to flaunt traditional dress codes. As one celebrant said:

[Same-sex] guys tend to be more outrageous. . . . I did one civil union and yeah they dressed in completely outrageous outfits, one of their friends was a designer and designed them these. . . . They looked, they had great high heeled boots so like platform boots and they wore, and they had sort of like fur cloaks and huge hats, big huge hats, but they weren't feminine at all. These were two very masculine guys.

Indeed, most of the comments about unusual or outrageous outfits pertained to same-sex civil unions.

Expressions of Love in the Ceremony

Many participants were encouraged by celebrants to express their feelings quite openly when exchanging their wedding vows and to talk about what their partner meant to them. Several participants mentioned that their celebrant asked them to write their own vows but to keep them secret from each other until the wedding day. For example, a married woman in her forties, who already had a child with her partner, talked about their ceremony:

> Neither of us knew what the other one was going to say until the day. . . . We had some bits that we did together, so we had a Leonard Cohen song . . . the lyrics that we said to each other and then . . . I found the Inuit wedding vow or Inuit song or something like that, something that people use in weddings quite a lot, but it was absolutely beautiful. It just fitted exactly how I felt and I can't really remember what else I said.

Later in the interview, she recalled the promises she had made:

> I think I promised to love him forever and I thought about that for a very long time and I felt confident that I could do that safely and that would probably be about all I promised to do, I think. I think I talked a lot about how good he was for me and all the stuff he'd done for me and everything. Yeah, promising to love him and love our child forever probably would have been about it in terms of promising to do actual things.

Vows were personalized by participants entering both marriage and civil unions. For example, an older lesbian woman spoke of their vows:

> It wasn't the traditional vows either but it was about being there for each other and also acknowledging what we mean, what we are to each other. Like I said to [partner] that she was my rock, that she felt very solid and she was really present and I think she said I was like the sea. 'Cause . . . what we've built over the years is this emotional depth that the ceremony just allowed us to get to another level that none of us anticipated.

Similarly a middle-aged gay man spoke of his vows, written the night before the ceremony, as a heartfelt expression of his feelings for his partner:

> I actually incorporated, because I wrote him a very special poem when we were apart fifteen or sixteen years before, and I incorporated some verses from that into my vows and it was from the heart, it actually mostly written the night before because I really wanted to just use the actual feeling that I was feeling at the time and I write the best when I'm under stress. But yeah, I really promised that I would always be there.

Occasionally, the celebrants adopted a mediating role in this process, as this young heterosexual woman makes clear: "We kept our vows secret from each other until the ceremony and [celebrant] mediated. So basically she wrote back to me and said [partner's] are way more romantic than yours, to try and get some kind of balance. So that was quite good." These are only a few examples of the personalized ways that participants expressed their feelings of love during the wedding ceremony. Some also ensured that their vows resisted traditional patriarchal practices, which is discussed in the next section.

Resisting Patriarchal or Inequitable Vows

First, we need to reiterate that many of the participants in our study had a university education and the sample included more women than men and a disproportionate number of people who had civil unions (including some different-sex couples). These factors might have increased the number of comments about patriarchal practices. Second, it is important to be aware that many of the churches and registry offices years ago removed the word *obey* from the bride's traditional promise to "love, honour, and obey" the groom. Nevertheless, in the participants' stories about their wedding, many of those in different-sex couples mentioned that they had dispensed with this practice, as well as the bride's father "giving her away" to the groom.

Some participants accepted the conventional religious cere-mony presented by their minister but nonetheless expected to retain gender equality in their ceremony. For example, a young Christian woman who cohabited for six years before marriage and had a "destination wedding" on a Pacific island beach with a local minister said: "We just used the vows that the minister had written and they just sounded quite nice but my main thing that I really didn't want to have in there was anything that was sort of against equality in the marriage so it was really important that everything was talking about equal partners."

Participants could not always remember what they promised in their ceremonial vows. For example, a young married woman who had cohabited for eight years before marriage described her wedding in a downtown church: "There was no honour and obey, that was definitely *not* in there. To love and cherish, I think there was respect and the standard richer and poorer, better and worse, things like that. I can't quite remember." Another married woman in her forties talked about her vows: "I would have said a lot of nice things about how much I loved him and all that sort of stuff yeah. I certainly *didn't* promise to obey him."

In the wedding vows, the importance of independence and mutual support were mentioned by this young woman entering a same-sex civil union:

I think the most important thing that we promised was that we would support each other's individuality and support each other to achieve what we want to achieve in life and try to main-tain independence. As much as we want to be together all the time, we know that that's not the most healthy way to have a relationship so we were really clear about wanting to just sup-port each other to do what we want to do in life and just al-ways be there, to be honest and faithful and just love each other unconditionally through whatever happens really. I guess that was the gist of it.

A man about thirty years old, who was about to enter a different-sex civil union, echoed this belief in the importance of independence in "marriage":

> There's the bit which is the "to have and to hold" tradition from this day forth for better or for worse. So we're just changing it for like "better or for more awesome" and things like that. Then we are going to have a section where we write our own vows, which is probably a cue for me to start thinking about it. But yeah essentially . . . I suppose it's about being together and being myself and her being herself and just enjoying each other's company.

Many heterosexual women in our study also resisted being "given away" by their father. In fact, some celebrants told us that they refused to ask the bride's family: "Who gives this woman away?" Instead, they typically asked the parents (or their friends or children) if they supported the marriage. The woman above who married in a downtown church after eight years of living together said: "Well my dad did walk me down the aisle . . . but there was no kind of verbal passing on." Another woman planning to enter a different-sex civil union commented:

> I'm not being given away because I am nearly thirty and I don't think I need to be given away. I've never been particularly fond of that but we've incorporated something into the service where all of our parents promise to support us through our relationship and that's the part that they play and that's equal amongst both our parents.

Especially the participants with divorced parents attempted to involve additional family members in the ceremony, such as their parents' new partners. A married woman about thirty years old talked about their wedding ceremony:

> One of my sisters did a reading. One of my other sisters signed the register. [Partner's] brother also signed the register. All the parents were included . . . [Partner's] parents are divorced and so there was a point in the ceremony where the minister asked whether the parents supported the marriage and all six stood up and said: "We do!"

In an interesting reworking of the tradition of giving the bride away, a Māori gay man in our study talked of being received into each other's families during the ceremony:

> In an English ceremony normally the bride is given away . . . and so we decided we'll have a receiving process, and so my sister stood and publicly received [partner] and had a public statement of receiving [partner] into my family and so he sort of crossed over and then [partner's] mother stood and publicly received me on behalf of their family, so I crossed over. So it was a receiving process rather than the giving away. So our families received the other into the family. I think that's a really important part too, it was a vital part of the ceremony.

Another tradition involves the bride and groom not seeing each other before the ceremony on their wedding day, which probably originated from the days of arranged marriages. Certainly this would have been easier when brides and grooms resided with their parents before marriage but now that most couples cohabit, this tradition is more difficult to maintain as one partner would have to stay in a hotel or with friends or family. Nevertheless, without being asked about this in the interview, several participants volunteered information about making an effort to maintain or break this tradition, occasionally with an interesting twist. For example, one woman in a same-sex civil union talked about breaking the tradition of seeing her partner before the ceremony on the wedding day: "We did an insemination on that day, a pregnancy insemination. . . . So that's why we saw each other on the day. Otherwise I don't think we would have because she stayed somewhere else the night before. Weird, eh?"

A gay man also spoke spontaneously about spending the night before the wedding apart from each other as part of his story about the incorporation of different cultural traditions into their ceremony:

> On the day we did a European traditional start to it where the groom normally goes to the bride's house and knocks three times on the door and then he's let in to see the bride and they go to the church or the registry office together. So we were staying in the same hotel but we didn't see each other, we didn't spend the night together the night before. We got ready separately and then I went downstairs and knocked, being the European person, knocked on the door and then [partner's] sister opened the door and I went in and saw him for the first time. We went in separate cars though and arrived together [at the house where the ceremony was to be held].

We found it particularly interesting that same-sex couples would choose to maintain this particular wedding tradition because it indicates that the original reason for traditional wedding practices is not always salient to decisions about whether or not to continue with the practice.

Including Children in the Ceremony

A number of participants in our study had children, stepchildren, and grandchildren, and these were sometimes asked to participate in their ceremony. For example, one mother reported: "[Child] was part of the ceremony as well. That was quite important to us, although at the same time it was very clearly our wedding, because he was part of the family." Another mother talked about the role of their child in the wedding:

> Our son was also our ring bearer so he had the rings for us in his pocket and because he's still little-ish, he's seven but still quite young to be responsible for something like that, my sister kind of had him with her and keeping an eye on things so that he didn't suddenly bolt off at the right moment or drop the rings or something. So he had our rings and he brought them to the minister when it was time for us to do the ring bit.

Most of the same-sex couples in our study did not have children, although several of the younger couples were actively seeking to become parents and to create families. There was, however, a middle-aged gay couple in the study who had been the foster parents of a large number of children in their community and extended family. One member of this couple said that their oldest boy spontaneously broke into a haka[2] as a tribute to them at the wedding:

> And our boy, who was seventeen at that point, he and his friends did a huge haka in honour of us when we were pronounced Mr and Mr [hyphenated names], because we've hyphenated our names now. And he and his friends launched into the most amazingly huge haka in front of everyone at the ceremony too. It was amazing.

Those having second weddings were more likely to include children in the ceremony. One of the celebrants commented that:

> [Second weddings] tend to include their children a lot more. . . .
> Like a wedding I did at the museum, the stepdaughter of the bride did a reading in the wedding and the stepson of the bride,

---

2.   A Maori welcoming ceremony that involves coordinated steps and chanting.

so the son of the groom did a video to say welcome to the family
and that sort of thing.

Several other celebrants also noted that the ceremonies of first
and second marriages tend to be different: "Second marriages seem
to be fairly short ceremonies because they're more interested in
having a good function, and that's just the formality of it because
they really want their friends and family together to have the do at
the night time."

The traditional practice of taking a wedding trip becomes more
difficult for parents with young children. In our study, a mother
with a preschooler commented:

> I guess the honeymoon bit was going away and spending a night
> in a luxurious lodge together, but when you've got a two and a
> half year old you can't really disappear to Hawaii for ten days,
> and we'd just bought the house as well. Oh that was how we or-
> ganized the honeymoon. We didn't ask for wedding presents, we
> asked people to contribute *koha* [a financial donation] towards
> our honeymoon.

Some of the older cohabiting participants wanted to ensure
that their own or their partner's children approved of their marriage plans. For example, a woman over sixty years old, who recently
married her long-term male partner, mentioned that her partner's
previous "wives" and their adult children had all expressed approval
of their marriage in emails they sent. In fact, her partner's son had
encouraged them to marry years before they actually did. The participant mentioned that this "external validation" was important to
her, perhaps because her male partner had delayed legal marriage
for so long.

Clearly, there were many variations in who was included in
wedding ceremonies, what the participant wore, and how they
celebrated the event. One celebrant in our study talked about the
variations this way:

Everyone is different and . . . some people want things like, you know, to have their dogs involved or to have their children involved. . . . they maybe might want to have a bit of humour in their ceremony. They might want to promise to share the remote or to be supportive when you go shopping every weekend or, you know, they want to make it a fun thing, not a rigid kind of structured thing that they have no say in.

This comment aptly summarizes the growing desire for personalized weddings in jurisdictions like New Zealand that permit independent celebrants to marry couples almost anywhere. However, creating this unique and elaborate event can be very stressful, especially for same-sex couples.

Wedding Stress

Most participants in our interviews, irrespective of their sexual orientation, talked about weddings as celebratory but stressful events that can exacerbate existing tensions between partners about whether, when, and how to formalize their relationship. Participants also mentioned disagreements with families about their choice of partner, the timing of the wedding, the venue, the details of the ceremony, and who was included or excluded from the guest list, and disagreements with friends about becoming a guest or an official witness. Other activities in the participants' lives also exacerbated the stress involved in planning the wedding. These included an unexpected pregnancy, starting a new job, finishing a university degree, buying a first home, arranging two wedding ceremonies, travelling to another location for the ceremony, and undergoing fertility treatment on the day of the wedding. Participants also told about wedding days disrupted by torrential rain or the absence of key family members.

Some participants made complicated wedding arrangements in distant locations, sometimes involving two separate ceremonies. One ceremony fit the legal requirements while the other was typically called the "real" wedding because it included more friends, family, and social recognition. For example, one woman who had been cohabiting for over seven years at the time of her marriage told us about her (non-legal) wedding with friends and family in the western United States when she was twenty-five years old and six months pregnant, before rushing to the eastern United States to pick up her older male partner's divorce papers from his previous marriage. This enabled them to legally marry there before she started graduate school. The non-legal "real" wedding took place on a west coast beach with personalized vows, photographs, friends, and family, and she reported that she wore a non-traditional blue seashell-patterned dress while her partner wore white shorts and a white shirt. The legal wedding in eastern America was solemnized by the town mayor in the gardens of the university with two witnesses. As she was seven months pregnant, she wore a stylish maternity dress and used the standard wedding vows, only striking out the "obey" clause. Four friends but no parents attended the legal wedding. Clearly, travelling from one side of the country to the other before starting a doctorate, while in the latter stages of pregnancy, must have been stressful.

Another example of complicated arrangements came from a man just over thirty years old who has been cohabiting for six years with his female partner. He told us about their forthcoming wedding in Germany, which they were planning via telephone and email. Because they were immigrants to New Zealand and all their family and many friends lived in Europe, they were planning to return to their home town to marry. Although they wanted to marry in his parents' garden, he reported that this has not been legally possible in Germany, where couples have historically been permitted to marry only in a church or registry office. In reply to our question about stress, he talked at length about planning two separate ceremonies while the marriage laws were in a state of flux:

> There's a formal part . . . which is going to be with our four best mates, bridesmaid and the family that will rock up on the registry office and do the old paperwork in the morning. So that's a very

bureaucratic act and that doesn't really mean anything to us at all. Hence the reason that we're doing the "actual marriage" . . . [the next day] at my parent's place. They have an old mansion and a huge garden with a seven hundred year old beech tree and under that tree we'll be exchanging our vows in front of all our friends and family . . . one hundred people roundabout. Then we're going to have a smoking hot party and that's us. Four weeks later we're going to fly back to winter.

However, at the time of our interview, the German law was changing to permit ceremonies outside the registry office, and they were trying to arrange for someone to do the official ceremony in the garden, a process that added to their stress because of the uncertainty entailed.

Although most weddings involve some level of anxiety, most of the participants reporting significant partner or family stress were entering civil unions rather than marriage. The sheer workload of preparing for a wedding while other aspects of their lives were changing seemed to place a great deal of pressure on some. For example, one woman under thirty talked about all the things that were happening in their lives while planning their same-sex civil union and the negative impact this had on their relationship:

We actually fought a lot coming up in to the time that we actually had our civil union, because I was on hormone therapy. I had started a new job. I had finished an incredibly stressful job that I'd had to leave because of issues around . . . workplace bullying and stuff. So we were in a very stressful state in that month before the wedding and we went at it hammer and tongs sometimes—just purely because we were stressed and we had a lot on. We had also had this really big New Year's Eve celebration that didn't help matters because that was like say four or five weeks before the wedding. . . . Like there was really nothing that we should have been kind of arguing over. It was just a feeling of like: "Oh my God, I've got so much to do!" And: "Have you done this? Well why not?"

Other participants also talked about having arguments with their partners in the lead-up to their weddings. These clashes usually revolved around the costs of the event or the work involved in the preparations. For instance, a middle-aged gay man of European ancestry who married his long-term Māori partner said:

> I sometimes found myself saying: "No we can't afford that," and getting a bit stressed because I don't like always being the person saying no. But some of the things I thought we can't afford that, it would have been fantastic to do that but I don't think we can afford that. Also running interference with my European family who were saying: "Oh well, you know that's too many people coming, you need a proper guest list and cross some of those people off . . ." There were a few times during the preparation where we got so stressed and ended up yelling at each other, and I was thinking is this worth it?

One source of conflict between couples involves sharing the preparatory work for the wedding. One young man we interviewed spoke of his failure to shoulder a fair share of the preparatory work:

> I suppose there's a lot of pressure for people to get things right. . . . It's a lot of concentration on the visual set up of the whole thing. Yeah just seems a bit over the top to me. So I suppose we've potentially had issues about me being a little bit blasé about that sort of stuff. And also potentially not being the normal sort of groom, and not really realizing the amount of work which is going on in the background to get a lot of this stuff to happen. But that sort of came to a head and I realized that I actually had to [do my fair share] . . . so yeah we had a confrontation about the fact that I wasn't pulling [my weight].

This man's story is in keeping with the findings of Humble et al. (2008) that brides are responsible for the vast majority of the wedding planning work in heterosexual couples.

Some of the circumstances that interviewees reported as stressful sounded relatively minor, such as this young woman's discussion of her partner's outfit for their civil union, which she thought was inappropriate:

> He sort of had this whole thing in his head of exactly what he wanted to be wearing and he wouldn't budge from it. In the end we had to get him a waistcoat specially made so probably his outfit was the most expensive thing. Yeah I was just trying really hard to just not lose my temper with it because I just thought it was over the top and no one was going to notice. Everyone looks at the bride anyway. I was trying really hard and most of the time I think I managed to keep calm but it was really, really frustrating.

She went on to say that she had to organize most of the wedding details herself and keep them a secret because her male partner was so fussy about the details.

One of the more challenging situations surrounding weddings concerned how to manage divorced and remarried parents and their new families. For example, a recently married woman around thirty years old referred to the stress involved in inviting her father's partner, with whom she did not get along:

> I invited my dad and his wife and their two children. . . . I don't think we've ever really had a strong relationship with them but I wanted them to be there. . . . So my husband and I invited the four of them, my dad, my step mum and my two half siblings. . . . For a time dad said yes he would attend, his wife wouldn't, but he would attend and the children would attend which would be nice and even suggested that they be involved in some way in the ceremony . . . .And so then they were going to, the three of them would attend, and then as it got closer and closer none of them were going to attend, and then eventually on the day my dad was there but that was sort of last minute I think, somebody giving him a nudge from his side of the family. So it was a bit of a battle.

Clearly not all participants wanted the stress of planning a big public wedding. Some preferred to have a small private ceremony that involved little organization but their partner wanted something more elaborate, which created additional stress. A middle-aged woman in a same-sex relationship talked about the stressful negotiations with her partner:

> My ideal would have been for me and [partner] to have eloped, run away and to have had a celebrant that we'd never met before and me and [partner] at the civil union and that's it, no one else. That would have been my ideal so I wanted it to be entirely invisible to the world and just end up with a piece of paper on the wall which is what I wanted. [Partner] wanted a ceremony and the whole shebang so it was a very difficult negotiation about how you do this stuff of seeking to respect each other's wishes and at the same time getting what we wanted which was really different. So the plan morphed over time.

This couple ended up with a compromise solution that limited the number of guests at the civil union ceremony to twenty close friends and family, followed by a party for seventy guests. This participant's desire for a quiet ceremony may have reflected her personality but also her attempt to reduce negative family reactions relating to her sexual orientation and civil union.

Particularly participants entering civil unions had to justify their decision to family and friends. While different-sex couples reported that they had to explain their unorthodox decision, some same-sex couples talked of family and friends who were ambivalent about or downright oppositional to their sexual orientation, their same-sex partner, and/or making all this public through formalization. Celebrants who presided over civil unions talked more than the other celebrants about the tensions and conflicts surrounding weddings, such as this older gay minister who was discussing same-sex civil unions:

Sometimes they might have an elderly relative who suddenly gets difficult. . . . You know, great aunts who have tut-tutted but gone along with it and then get all self-righteous. . . . With same-sex marriages, the family might have tolerated them being lesbian or gay or bi, but then see the ceremony as flaunting their sexuality . . . or as somehow being sacrilegious or disrespectful to marriage, and they will again vote with their feet in not coming. That's very painful.

A middle-aged lesbian celebrant, who performed only civil unions, highlighted the high level of family tension surrounding same-sex weddings, to the point where she now takes pre-emptive action:

I've actually got to the point where I now sometimes say: "Tell me what land mines are out there. I need to know who's potentially going to be a problem and what those problems are. . . . I don't want to blunder in." I don't want to unknowingly put them under pressure and I also need to be aware that on the day some people misbehave.

The same-sex couples reported a number of stressful issues relating to their civil unions, which one lesbian spoke of a prime example of "hetero-normativity" in action. This woman, who was under thirty years old, told a long story about her exclusion from the wedding of her partner's cousin and how she did not want this man at her civil union:

I was really upset as well because [partner's] really good cousin had gotten married to this guy and they hadn't invited me to the wedding despite the fact that we were fully engaged at the time of the wedding. But yet we had to invite them to our wedding. . . . So I was kind of going: "Why the f--- are we inviting people to our wedding that didn't want me at theirs?" Yeah. So I remember now that actually caused a big fight, actually days before the wedding.

Because they flew in from Australia, and [partner] was going to spend time with them and I was like: "I don't want you spending time with them right now! Things are stressful, they don't give a shit about me kind of thing and I'm only inviting them because they are family but I don't even want them here." So I suppose that kind of caused tensions.

The same woman also talked about her perception of the lack of respect for same-sex civil unions compared to heterosexual marriages:

The other thing that people did that I don't think they would have done for a wedding, just remembering stressful things, is getting dressed, into my wedding dress and getting texts from people saying: "Oh sorry, I can't make your wedding, have a good day doll," that kind of thing. And I was kind of like I'm sure you wouldn't do this if this was an actual wedding, you know *marriage wedding*. You know what I mean? And also people RSVP'ing on Facebook and saying, days before the wedding: "Oh, sorry I can't make it anymore, one of my kids is sick," and stuff like that. I knew it was kind of stuff that they would not even try if they were going to a wedding.

Celebrants and cohabitants both mentioned disagreements with friends within the gay/lesbian communities about the wisdom of civil unions. Some same-sex participants expected, but did not always receive, support from their gay and lesbian friends. For example, one woman invited her lesbian friend to become a bridesmaid or witness in her same-sex civil union but the friend refused, saying that she wanted nothing to do with civil unions. This interaction was clearly very distressing for her:

I only had one friend that was going to come to the civil union. I asked her if she would be my witness, except I used crap language. I said: "Would you be my bridesmaid?" and she said no, she wouldn't be my witness, she wouldn't be a signatory and that she would have nothing to do with civil unions. It was devastating. I was so upset, I was devastated and I never sat down and explained why I was having a civil union . . . . It was hugely damaging and very upsetting and I was profoundly distressed and disturbed. So I asked my sister, so that meant that my friend wasn't invited to the civil union.

Given a context of opposition and hostility toward same-sex civil unions, gay and lesbian couples often expect a certain amount of tension and conflict. For instance, a middle-aged gay man refused to invite his "homophobic" father to his civil union, even though he was encouraged to by his partner. However, some stories suggested unanticipated levels of social acceptance by relatives and heterosexual colleagues. A secular celebrant recounted the story of a couple she recently joined in civil union, where the woman was nervous about "coming out" with her work colleagues:

One of her colleagues found out about the civil union and they gave her a wedding shower and . . . they were all talking about it, what are you wearing and they've all got that whole buzz going on that happens around weddings. And she was just gobsmacked because she had not expected them to be supportive like that. And so for her it was a kind of second coming out . . .

This same celebrant told another story about family acceptance of a same-sex civil union but at a level that may have been over-exuberant:

We worked with a couple who had been together for seven years and their families had never met. . . . They were not "out" to any of their neighbours or anything . . . but many closets are made of glass and they thought they would have a ceremony with just themselves and a couple of friends. By the time it got to the day their families had come fully on board. They'd thrown them a huge engagement party. . . . They were doing the tuxedos, the full gowns. . . . There was bridesmaids and page boys and God knows what else, and flower girls doing their thing. It was the full production and they were astounded and it kind of swept them away in a wave of family expectation and involvement because their families were just waiting for the opportunity to become accepting and this was their excuse.

These examples illustrate that same-sex couples are sometimes surprised at the level of heterosexual acceptance. Yet their surprise is indicative of a social context where same-sex couples are primed to anticipate opposition to their choice of partner and the very idea of legalizing their relationships. Opposition, as we have shown, is not confined to heterosexual family and friends, but also includes gay and lesbian friends who see civil unions as mirroring the ills of heterosexual marriage or see civil unions as a "second-class marriage."

Conclusions

The prevalent idea that weddings should reflect personal values and lifestyle has encouraged many couples to view their wedding as unique and memorable, an event that announces who they are in terms of social class, sexual orientation, and lifestyle aspirations. The trend for couples to pay for much of their own wedding and pressure from popular culture and the "wedding industry" help to explain why weddings have become increasingly personalized, expensive, and elaborate. Older and financially independent couples command a stronger negotiating position with their respective families but they often must negotiate with each other about whether or not to formalize, the type of event to host, and how much money to spend. In our study, personalized weddings were expected by participants of all age groups, for both marriages and civil unions, and for same-sex and different-sex couples. However, some of the most non-traditional weddings were civil unions between gay men and older couples who had initially been opposed to legalizing their relationships.

Despite the international trend to personalized weddings, some English-speaking jurisdictions continue to limit who is authorized to marry couples and where marriages can take place. Some also restrict marriage to heterosexual couples while permitting same-sex couples to enter into civil unions or civil partnerships. Other jurisdictions provide no opportunity for same-sex couples to legalize their relationships, although some couples in those places have chosen to have marriage-like commitment ceremonies. New Zealand is an example of a country that added a new form of legal relationship as a political compromise to the opposition to same-sex marriage, before same-sex marriage was legalized in 2013. Civil unions are more inclusive as they can involve different-sex or same-sex couples.

Despite widespread secularization of society and emphasis on the importance of personal choice, many marriage and civil union ceremonies continue to include traditional symbols of patriarchal and heterosexual marriage, even when they involve same-sex couples and people with non-traditional values. In our interviews, several celebrants expressed surprise and annoyance at the traditional wedding practices of so many of their couples, reporting that only a minority seriously attempt to transform the ceremony. Yet, the couples themselves often redefine these symbolic practices to fit their values and preconceptions of a "real" wedding, which tend to reflect representations from magazines, television, celebrity weddings, and other aspects of popular culture.

CHAPTER 5

Does Formalization Really Make a Difference?

Introduction

Studies from several English-speaking countries have concluded that marriage not only provides slightly more legal rights than cohabitation but that marriage has retained much of its symbolic value. When cohabiting couples marry or formalize their relationship in a civil union or civil partnership, they make public their already private commitment. Other people often view this as a "rite of passage" or an act of maturity or greater commitment, the creation of a new durable family unit, or provision of a more secure environment for raising children (Cherlin 2010; Kirby 2008; Sassler and Miller 2011; Steele et al. 2005). Previous research also suggests that same-sex couples who decide to formalize their relationships expect that "marriage" will provide them with a stronger sense of belonging, better links with kin, and greater respect and acknowledgement for their relationships (Schecter et al. 2008; Shipman and Smart 2007).

In our study, most participants who had already formalized their relationship reported some level of change, either in their relationship or the way that others treated them. They typically said that their marriage or civil union made them feel more secure emotionally, that others viewed their relationship as more durable, and parents and older relatives were more accepting of their partner as a family member. Those who reported that "marriage" had made a notable difference included participants of all ages and backgrounds but was more prominent among those females who were part of same-sex couples, participants with strong religious values, and those who were parents or were planning to become parents.

Some participants mentioned that formalization made little difference to them but that certain significant people in their lives thought that it made a difference. A small number of participants (mainly men) reported that formalization had made no difference at all, even though they had agreed to marry. This latter group typically contained participants who were persuaded to formalize their relationship by their partner.

The rest of this chapter is divided into four parts based on our participants' perceptions of the impact of formalization and drawing on their verbatim comments. The first section focuses on those who claimed that marriage or civil union made a notable difference to their intimate relationship. The second section focuses on changes to identity following formalization. The third section discusses participants who mention minor differences but concentrates on changes in how others respond to couples following formalization. The fourth part focuses on participants who said formalization made no difference.

Formalization Makes a Notable Difference to the Couple

Most of our participants who had already formalized their relationship said that they now felt different—usually more secure, "settled," or "mature." People of all ages made these comments, but particularly the participants who were part of same-sex couples talked about the importance of gaining legal rights, acknowledgement, and social recognition for their relationship. For example, a woman in her fifties, who recently entered a same-sex civil union after twenty-one years of cohabitation, talked about feeling more secure and spoke of the symbolic nature of formalization:

> It definitely makes me feel that we have taken our relationship into a legal domain that has more rights, or more recognition possibly, and that we are honouring our relationship in a more committed way. . . . In your community, with your friends, with your family, it tells people that this relationship is a committed long-term relationship.

Many couples in our study created personalized vows that made explicit their love and long-term commitment. The female partner of the above woman also commented that the civil union ceremony itself had provided an opportunity for both of them to talk about how they experienced their love for each other, which she described as a memorable learning experience and a "profound gift." In addition, she mentioned that formalizing same-sex relationships produced written records of gay and lesbian relationships that previously did not exist:

> I think that in genealogy, gays and lesbians don't exist because there is no paper trail of the relationships. There's a paper trail for enduring *heterosexual* relationships and the children, and then gays and lesbians in history in genealogy are invisible . . . [Partner's] and my relationship is not invisible in the future. It existed as a relationship, as a connection between the two families and it is there to be seen. . . . I think my mother would register that on some level, but I'm not sure that anyone else in the family would.

This same woman also talked about the importance of shared memories of the civil union:

> I think there's something about reflecting back, having the photos, having had a wonderful time and declaring our love in public. I think that that has a memory which we look back on fondly but I *don't* think it changed our relationship. I think it is part of our memories.

A man in his forties, also in a same-sex relationship, argued that having a civil union had made a big difference to his life:

> There are many people who say that after marriage or whatever there's no difference. I think rubbish, there's huge difference. When I say difference, it's not about better, it's just raised the

level. It's enhanced the relationship. It's honoured the relationship. . . . I feel I have a greater responsibility to our relationship now and I feel that I will even though I'm strong about who we are and who I am, I feel much more stronger about it and I will politically, or whatever it takes, stand my ground about our relationship. . . . It's easy to sometimes want to give up on it when you're having bad times, when you're not happy with each other. When you're not seeing things at the same way, it's easy to give up and the civil union is another anchor that says to us we have too much to give up on.

This man also talked about the significance of creating a historical trace of same-sex relationships through the process of legalization:

I'm not the first to be gay in my genealogy, I'm not the first . . . and I certainly won't be the last and so it's really important that what [partner] and I are doing is ensuring that those generations that follow us will have a safe life ahead of them. I expect that when we die there will be very clear records of our love and our part in our family so the generations that follow when there are gay, lesbian, changed gender people who will be in our *whanau* [extended family] they will know that it's safe to be so. To me that's important. That's our legacy besides the love, our legacy is to ensure that all those who will be as we are in the generations to follow will be supported in our family.

A young woman in her twenties, also in a same-sex civil union, argued that her relationship had changed since formalization:

I think our relationship is better because I think it's, well, it's not better because our relationship was always good, but I think it's more secure and it's stronger. Yeah. I'm less likely to take off if we have an argument or something. I'm more likely to just stick around, because it's like what's the point.

Heterosexual participants in our study also believed that formalization had made a difference, sometimes unexpectedly. For example, a heterosexual woman in her mid-thirties said that she had not expected any change after their civil union because it was just an excuse for a party. However, she reported that the relationship had changed:

> We sort of thought we were really just having a party and just a way to get our parents to chip in to a piss up kind of thing and keep them happy at the same time. But I think it has actually changed things. . . . But I think we both do feel a bit more—it feels more solid somehow. It's really odd. I'm really surprised by that, because I would never have thought that things felt transient or insubstantial beforehand. But something about making that kind of public declaration, I think. Maybe that aspect is more important than the . . . legal kind of thing.

A number of participants expressed surprise by the change they experienced after formalization. For example, a heterosexual man in his early forties, who had recently married following an eight-year cohabitation with his partner, during which time they had a child and bought a house together, said that he was surprised that he felt more relaxed and comfortable following their marriage:

> Afterwards we found out we were a bit more relaxed about our commitment for some reason. We just feel a bit more comfortable with each other after we've been married. I'm not exactly sure why. I think maybe it's the process of going through this marriage ceremony. We seem to be a bit more relaxed with each other. That was quite surprising. I wasn't expecting that. I just didn't think anything would change really, but it did.

A man in his early thirties, who is married to a woman in her late thirties, talked about the way people perceive married couples, referring also to his wife's opinion:

I think people still think that there's a certain kind of serious-
ness or something of the relationship that comes from getting
married and [partner] said that she thinks people see us differently now, like in the way that my parents relate to her and stuff.
I think they maybe take the relationship more seriously or things
like that, which is kind of interesting.

Participants also referred to marriage as an indicator of maturity. For example, a married mother in her forties, whose mother
divorced her first husband in order to marry this woman's father,
suggested that cohabitation is appropriate for younger people but
marriage is a social symbol of adulthood or maturity:

I think when you're twenty-five and you're living with someone,
we took it more as there's no difference between married and living together and I think most of my friends felt the same way. I
think now . . . at a certain age it's sort of thought, "Well, grow up
and get married!"

Later in the interview, however, she reported that her relationship had changed after marriage and had become more "secure,"
speaking of marriage as a "rite of passage."

Finally, another young woman who recently married in a religious ceremony talked about the importance of marriage for both
men and women when she said: "There's kind of like a stereotype
that it's just the women that want to get married. But I don't think
that's true. A lot of the men really want that stability and stuff as
well, and if you've made the decision to get married, the relationship has more stability . . . ."

Claims that marriage enhanced feelings of security may well be
connected to making a public commitment as part of the formalization process. According to Stanley et al. (2006), making a public
commitment enhances feelings of dedication between partners—
dedication commitment—but also enhances how *tied* partners are
to each other—constraint commitment (Stanley et al. 2006). Being

committed to each other means that couples imagine their future in collective terms, as lives entwined together. For a man in his early thirties, who was about to get married to his partner of six years, an imagined future together was an important difference between cohabitation and marriage, with marriage providing a more suitable foundation for joint projects:

> It shows that you are committed to a long-term future . . . with that person and it's almost like a kind of basement or building block for you to say: "Well we're here now, we've got this together . . . " and it gives you like foundation . . . . It's something you can build from. . . . For me when we were together as a couple and cohabitating . . . I don't think we'd actually really created a vision for the two of us together long term. It was a lot about here and now, what are we trying to achieve short maybe medium term, but not long term. And I think marriage is about that long-term prospect.

Several other men in our study who were in different-sex relationships also linked formalization with a promised future together and the possibility of joint projects like buying a house: "I think our relationship will change [with formalization] in the sense that our goals will change. That we'll start looking towards a house, that we'll start looking towards getting that all nailed down."

Both different-sex and same-sex participants indicated that their increased sense of security was also attributable to the requirement marriage imposes on couples to tolerate each other's personal flaws and to work through conflict. For example, in response to a question about whether formalization had made a difference to her, a heterosexual woman who had been married for three years said: "I just instantly felt more secure. You know he can't run away now, and has to put up with the PMT,[1] I can go back to being my

---

1.   Premenstrual tension.

horrible self after six months of being nice. Yeah more secure." In response to the same question another woman, who had become a mother of three young children following her marriage, said:

> I guess the difference is that . . . if you're going through issues or a hard time in your relationship, I think that maybe being married just makes you stop and think that little bit more. . . . Prior to being married we had these horrible fights where I would throw all his clothes out the house and the dramatic blah, blah, blah. . . . But we have a rule since we got married that you don't even joke about the D word, divorce. So for me I guess there is this thing that because we're married now you don't even call into question, that's not even an option. . . . I do wonder if maybe being married just makes you stop and think that little bit more because there is that kind of added legality issue about if you were to end things, things would be that much more difficult from that side of things.

These replies suggest that marriage for many of our participants was seen to increase feelings of security through reducing the sense of the contingency of relationships. In other words, marital relationships are supposed to withstand the everyday challenges of domestic life and are not supposed to be dissolved on a whim. Or to put this slightly differently: when you become married you are no longer on trial, in contrast to cohabitation, which is often understood as a "trial marriage."

The possibility that marriage reduces relationship contingency is closely connected to what Andrew Cherlin (2004) calls enforceable trust: because marriage entails a public promise of a future together, partners can exert more pressure on each other to meet their relational commitments, safe in the knowledge that they are less likely to experience rejection in the form of separation. Such ideas go some way to explaining why legal marriages are statistically more durable than cohabitation relationships (Baker 2010).

Formalization and Changes to Identity

A number of participants connected the formalization of their relationships to changes in identity and to new forms of interaction between them as a couple. Unsurprisingly, given that surname change following marriage is a highly gendered custom, women in different-sex relationships were more likely to reflect on issues relating to this practice than heterosexual men. But both different-sex and same-sex individuals spoke about name changes following marriage or civil union. The following quote comes from a recently married man in his early thirties who highlights the ongoing gendered implications for identity that follow from marriage:

> For women they're usually the ones who change their last name so they sort of make the mental change I think. I think the woman goes through the mental change a lot more than the man because the man he just generally carries on his life and then his partner will come to meet him in terms of grabbing his name and you know taking his children and stuff like that. Yeah I think it's more a mental change for the female in the relationship than the male.

While the custom has been for women to take a man's surname on marriage, name change for women on marriage is no longer a foregone conclusion, especially among those with university education (Hamilton, Geist, and Powell 2011). In our sample, in which highly educated people were over-represented, a large number of the women in different-sex relationships kept or planned to keep their own names. One woman in her early thirties, who had a traditional white wedding in a downtown church, was vehemently opposed to changing her surname and linked it to the loss of a woman's identity:

> I think that's the nice thing about civil unions because it kind of gives an option to people who don't want to have some of the negative connotations that can come along with the idea of

getting married and becoming the husband's property. Not ever having someone call you Mrs Blah Blah, which isn't actually your name, particularly Mrs husband's first name, like you have absolutely no identity. . . . I can't stand going to other people's weddings when they get introduced, like "welcome Mr and Mrs Mike Brown." I want to jump up and punch the bride in the face and tell her that she's not in the 1950s.

Other women in our study expressed less strong opinions on the matter, but still kept their surnames. For instance, another recently married young woman in her early thirties, who was studying for her second degree, said:

I kept my own surname. We didn't really kind of see a need and he was perfectly happy and I decided I'd rather keep mine. It's done me pretty well for thirty years. But also that's something you can change if you ever want to as well. So I can always change my mind about that down the track if I feel like it, but at this point in time I don't really feel that that is necessary.

Several women indicated that the question of name change was a source of internal reckoning and/or external pressure. For instance, one recently married woman, in her early forties, initially thought she would keep her birth name, but tells of having an epiphany that led to a change of heart:

I wasn't going to change my surname. I decided the morning I woke up after I got married that it was my last bastion of, I don't know, pig headedness. Defiance. And I wasn't going to because I thought [first name, surname] is my identity, that's what everybody knows me as professionally. And I woke up and I thought, "I can't put my heart 99 percent into a marriage, I want it to work, and I need to leave the old [surname] behind and I'm starting a new. This is a new track."

Another woman in her early sixties, whose husband had taken twelve years to propose to her, described being put under pressure by him, about a year after their marriage, to change her surname to his. Asked if she was changing her surname she said:

I'm in the process, I'm transitioning. And that's somewhat unlike me. [Current surname] is what I've had since 1975, it's my first husband's name and although [current husband] says, you change your name or not, there was one comment that he made, just a little while ago about "Well you haven't changed your name. You haven't taken the time." But I said, you know, "I intend to do it." And he said, "Yeah but you haven't." I mean the implication was: well if it was a priority you'd do that.

Participants in different-sex marriages also spoke about shifting from using *partner* to *wife* or *husband* as their preferred referent in the aftermath of their marriages. One recently married man in his forties clearly found the use of *wife* much simpler: "It's quite nice to be able to say this is my wife, it's just easy. It's an easy introduction and it's something that everyone understands. So everyone's got a common point or reference to it, I guess." Others talked about their intentions to replace *partner* with *husband* but forgetting to do so because *partner* just rolled off their tongues. This was the case for a woman in her early thirties, who had been married for two years and had a six-month-old child: "Like I still accidentally refer to [first name of husband] as my partner instead of my husband sometimes because I did it for so many years and I just forget."Another, more recently married woman, who had kept her surname, also spoke about forgetting to mark their change in status in public interactions through the use of the term *husband*:

I'm still calling myself by my name and he's still calling himself by his name. There's not really that many differences. . . . We call each other wife and husband when we remember. I constantly forget actually, introduce my partner as my partner: "Oh he's my husband." We still have the same kind of way of interacting that we normally did but we yeah tease each other about being husband and wife.

Interestingly, several of the same-sex couples in our study also spoke of surname change following their civil unions. One gay couple, who had been together for sixteen years and fostered numerous children from their extended family together, hyphenated their surnames, a change which caused them to feel even more integrated into each other's lives: "When you sign something or tell someone your name is Jim [partner's surname–own surname] now it's even more, I feel even more a part of his life even, more a part of his family now than I did before."

One of the lesbian couples also spoke about surname change in the context of wanting to have children together:

> We're trying to have children, and it's around . . . conforming to an idea of the heterosexual family, which again really doesn't sit easily with me. But I know at the same time I've got to make things easier for children . . . , which is why I've also changed my name since the civil union. . . . I changed my name . . . so that we would be seen as a family unit and you know, like yeah, very much subscribing to this heterosexual notion of what a family is, even though we don't really want to do that, but we kind of have to make it okay for our children.

Her partner explained their decision about who changed surnames as an outcome of different levels of attachment to their identities:

> [Partner] decided that she wanted to take my name because she wasn't particularly attached to her name as much as I was. She had changed her name previously from her birth father's name to her stepfather's name, so for me, my name, I'm quite attached

to it in terms of my identity. I don't know, it's kind of weird, but I just feel a lot more attached to my last name than what she did and so she was, yeah she just said one day that she wanted to change her name to [surname] and I was like, "yeah, sweet."

Formalization Made Minor Differences to Some Couples but Notable Difference to Others

A small number of our participants, both those with traditional and those with non-traditional values, reported that marriage made some difference to them, but the difference was rather intangible. For example, a man in his mid-forties in a same-sex civil union believed his relationship had changed following his civil union, although he had difficulty expressing the nature of this change:

> Yes, it has definitely changed. It feels more, well, it's always been a stable relationship but it feels, I just can't explain it. You just feel different. And both my partner and I know that it feels different and other friends who have done this also agree. It feels more formalized. . . . From a personal point of view it just formalizes what was a long-term and will continue to be a long-term relationship. But it doesn't worry us what other people think either way. So it's something that we did for ourselves, not anybody else.

Similarly another participant, a recently married woman in her early thirties, also struggled to put her finger on exactly what had changed in their relationship:

> It's funny because I think it has added something and I can't tell you what or why. But it feels slightly different. It feels just kind of, I guess maybe a bit deeper that there's a commitment that is there kind of. . . . And it's hard to say because I don't know that I didn't feel like that before, but there is something that feels different I think and yeah it's kind of hard to quantify. I think we are both quite glad that we did decide to do it.

However, many participants thought that the formalization of their partnerships had altered the way they or their partners were treated by others. A woman in her late twenties, who had recently entered a same-sex civil union, reported that formalization changed the way others viewed her sexually when she said: "I think that people are less likely to try and get in there with me, given that I am civilly unioned . . . the boundaries are more clear."

Other participants in the study located their changed treatment from others in terms of perceptions about the permanence or stability of their relationships. One recently married older woman, who had for many years sought an agreement from her partner to marry, outlined a developmental trajectory for relationships that she believed affected how her husband's now adult children reacted to her:

> Yeah, I think there were maybe four transitions. One was, "this is dad's new girlfriend" . . . so there was that initial stage. Then there was the stage of, "Okay, so now it's a little more than just a girlfriend" and "maybe she's not going to last long." And then there was the stage of, "she's not going away." And then there was the stage of marriage, "That she's not going away and they accept her." . . . So yeah I think they look at me differently.

Another woman in her late thirties, who had recently married, also said that formalization made a difference to their parents and siblings: "I do think my parents see cohabiting and marriage as different and I think my partner's parents do as well. I think they would probably see a civil union as different again, although I've never actually talked to them about it." This woman went on to describe some tricky interactions between her male partner and her more traditional sisters in the lead-up to the wedding, which reminded her of their different perspectives on cohabitation:

> When my sisters said things like: "Oh finally you'll be a proper brother-in-law" to my partner, I thought, he's been that for ten

years, come on. So there were definitely some little things that we both just had to wear and kind of not react to because the way we saw it and the way they saw it was never going to be exactly the same. We had been happily cohabitating without being married, and being completely committed to each other and seeing ourselves as a family for a long time. I do think they saw us in that way as well . . . but there would be the odd little comment that would just remind us of our different choices.

How others understand the difference between cohabitation and marriage seemed to be key to the different reactions and responses couples received following the formalization of their relationships, as another young woman in her early thirties in our study suggested:

I think maybe even when you're quite comfortable with things as they are when you're cohabitating, I think everybody's got people in their life who would take a legal union more seriously than a de facto union. So I think, yeah I think actually a major part of what's changed . . . particularly with [partner's] family, is that they feel so much more comfortable now, they kind of feel like we're settled and they don't need to worry about us and that's just quite nice. There's not this kind of underlying uncertainty on their part about what's going to happen. Is this serious or not?

A young man who was about to have a different-sex civil union also anticipated that older, more conservative members of their families would grant their relationship more recognition following their ceremony:

I think for some people it puts credence on your relationship. Like there are certain members of your family who would see that you're not together until you are married, the old school members of your family, the granddads and stuff like that. You know, when you're married then it's real.

Participants reported that it wasn't only family members who treated married couples differently from cohabiting partners. An educated mother in her forties, who recently married four years after having a child with her partner, talked about marriage influencing the way couples are viewed by helping professionals:

> I'm worst case scenario girl, I always think if something happened to one of us it's good that I can walk into a hospital and say "I'm his wife." I don't have to say his girlfriend or some other random thing. . . . It doesn't make any difference to us but I just think it makes a difference to how other people maybe see us.

In a separate interview, her husband, who comes from a minority cultural community, made a stronger case about the perceptions of others when he said:

> The advantage of marriage, I guess, is that formal level of legal recognition. You're just afforded a bit more recognition from society and institutions like sort of hospitals or police or, you know, any time you're dealing with any sort of institutional power or whatever, if you say you're married or this is my wife, it seems to provide a level of, I don't know, it makes the interaction easier. And it's also been beneficial for me for my family as well. It's improved my relationship with my family in terms of, not my immediate family, but my uncles and aunts. And I guess the wider [ethnic] community in [New Zealand city] where I'm from originally, there's that level of recognition and I guess it's, they see it as another stage of adulthood, I guess or growing or maturing.

The conferring of respectability through marriage was also noted by an older previously divorced woman, who married her long-term partner merely for immigration reasons: "When I was in [other country], I could say to any audience at all this is my husband, my husband is with me. . . . So it makes you generally more mainstream . . . gives you more respect." This woman's comments, like some of the others, points to the continued relevance of a moral distinction between marriage and cohabitation, which results in cohabitation being seen as an illicit and non-conformist living arrangement, albeit an arrangement that has become tolerated and widespread.

Yet the difference in treatment our participants describe following the formalization of their relationships is also clearly connected to a lingering uncertainty over the nature of their cohabiting relationships. As we mentioned in Chapter 1, cohabitation can mean a variety of things, from co-residential dating to an alternative to marriage, and this leads to a sense of ambiguity over the future of the relationship and the kinds of obligations that exist between partners. The ambiguous status of cohabiting relationships is compounded by the lack of ritual that surrounds moving in together, because this prevents the development of shared meanings, both among the couple and their family and friends, about the nature of the relationship. Moving from a private to a public commitment through the ritual of marriage puts an end to this ambiguity by securing an agreement between the couple in front of others of a long-term, if not permanent, future together.

Marriage/Civil Union Is No Different than Cohabitation

A small number of participants said that they didn't think that marriage or civil union made any difference to their relationship or to their treatment by others. Several people expressed some apprehension that marriage might have changed their relationships and were relieved to find that it had not. For instance the woman, who we mentioned above who remarried for immigration reasons, said:

> I mean I was a little worried that it might change the relationship
> or something. And I was a little worried because it seemed like
> making a concession. But in the end it was just like other things
> that you do when you're travelling you know. . . . And in fact I
> think both of us watched with suspicion to see if anything would

be worse and [husband] and I were sort of relieved when nothing changed.

For others, the claim that marriage or civil union had not had any effect on them or their relationship was an outcome of their rejection of marriage as a tie that constrained their actions. For still others, it was an outcome of both pleasurable and painful life events that had produced a strong sense of togetherness prior to marriage or civil union. For example, a married man in his late twenties, with a semi-professional occupation and no religious affiliation, lived with his female partner for six years before she convinced him to marry her. He reported that he came from a "broken family" and delayed the decision to marry because he was concerned about making the "right choice" and worried about the possibilities of divorce. However, he also said that he didn't think that marriage was important or made any difference. He had already told us the story of their "engagement" when they went to the bank for a loan and were offered more money than they needed for his new motorcycle. In front of the bank officer, his female partner said that if he could have his motorcycle, with the extra money she could have her ring, which he agreed to. When we asked about the reaction of family and friends to their "engagement," he said:

> They were all fairly stoked. Everyone is always happy to hear about a wedding. My mum instantly thought it would mean grandchildren. Little does she know that we're never really going to go down that road. . . . I got lots of congratulation texts and stuff like that which is quite funny because I'd told no one and yet I was getting all these congratulations. It was almost like ten minutes after we'd done it.

Apparently, his partner sent text messages to all their friends and family as soon as they left the bank that they were "engaged." When we talked to him in the interview about whether he felt that his relationship was different now that he was married, he commented that marriage did not make much difference except limiting his sex life and wearing a wedding ring:

> I've resisted a lot of my urges but . . . when you get married you kind of think "Right, I'm going to put on this ring and then every girl on the planet is going to look at me a different way and I'll look at them a certain different way," but it doesn't quite do that. . . . Yeah I don't know, I think you just think when you get married that things will change, but they don't . . . and that's fine. . . . So legally I suppose there are a few differences but in reality, being in a long-term de facto or long-term partnership yeah I suppose there are no real disadvantages to it insomuch as you are pretty much legally entitled to half the property and child rights and that stuff. They all stay the same. . . . So advantages to getting married, I suppose you know you get to wear a ring and that's pretty much it.

Another heterosexual man in his mid-forties, who cohabited for eight years before his relatively traditional wedding, said:

> I don't see any advantages or disadvantages [to marriage]. Like on a personal level, there is nothing that changes. We were together for ten years and to all intents and purposes we were together despite the fact that there's someone saying it's now legal. It doesn't matter to me. I was still committed to it all irrespective of whether someone says it's now legal or not.

A female participant in our study, who was in her twenties and in a same-sex relationship, spoke of a generational change with respect to attitudes toward marriage and same-sex relationships when she said:

> For friends and relatives around our age, marriage doesn't seem to be as important anymore, as crucial. They're all living with their partners and not married. And if people do get married, it's

awesome, great celebration, all that sort of stuff, but if they don't, it's not a big deal either.

There were other participants who spoke of the development of a strong sense of commitment to their partners as a result of shared experiences as a couple rather than the formalization. A number of different-sex participants said that having a child was a turning point in their relationships that reflected an increased commitment to each other and bound them together indefinitely. For instance, a heterosexual man who had become a father four years prior to getting married argued that having a child represented much more of a change in their relationship than marriage had, especially to the way that he and his wife managed their money:

> One of the significant things in our relationship other than getting married was having a child, so that changed the parameters of our relationship. So prior to that . . . we had separate money and separate income. If we bought anything like the fridge or couch we would both fork out of our own money, half for everything out of our respective incomes. But since we had the child . . . the money just became pooled. . . . We didn't have two separate incomes, we just had *an income*. . . . So there was a change. . . . We started recognizing things are more formal or defining things as a family.

Likewise, a woman in a different-sex relationship, who married when her first child was just over a year old, said that it was children—not marriage—that produced an unbreakable bond between herself and her husband: "I don't think marriage solidifies the relationship. To me it's more children that provide that unbreakable bond. I mean we are together through them and whatever happens, we sort of become tied." This woman went on to reject the notion of marriage as a permanent tie:

> I guess for me, marriage doesn't necessarily mean a permanent thing, and I've seen it too much . . . . It's not like thirty or forty

years ago where you stayed together until you die, quite often unhappily. I think people are more willing to walk away now, but for me, being married or not married doesn't necessarily mean I'm more likely to leave or less likely to break up.

She nonetheless wanted to get married during her pregnancy, in part because of her sensitivity to family disapproval of their un-wed status, but her partner was initially lukewarm about the idea. Eventually, they married and spent $10,000 on a relatively tradi-tional wedding, in which she made her wedding dress, several of the other dresses, and the wedding cake, even though she was also employed and caring for a young child. However, she argued that there was no real difference between marriage and cohabitation, and that her wedding was just an excuse for a party. When we asked if her parents or friends were pleased that they were getting mar-ried, she answered:

> No, the parents didn't care. The friends didn't care. It was just an excuse to get together and have a party. . . . I think cohabitation and marriage are the same. I mean it doesn't really matter in the long run whether you are married or not. . . . I think what matters is commitment of the people really and if you're not committed it doesn't matter if you are married or not.

For other participants, both same-sex and different-sex, it wasn't children that produced a strong sense of commitment but difficult life experiences. For example, a man in his fifties, who had a civil union in the registry office with his same-sex partner after cohabiting for nearly twenty years, reported no change in their re-lationship or in family acceptance of his partner, which has been positive for many years. When asked if the civil union changed his relationship, he answered:

> We've been together for a long time . . . there are many more things that we've done that have actually strengthened our relationship

that are not to do with getting civil united. I mean my parents both had spent a long time in old age in decline and in rest homes and it was all very, very hard work and [partner] held my hand all the way through that and [partner's] mother got cancer and she lived with us and we looked after her for a couple of years while she died here in this house. So those sorts of things are much more important in terms of the bond that we've got to each other because we've got a shared history . . . .

A woman who married her different-sex partner of seven years also attributed the strengthening of their relationship to the difficult times they had gone through prior to the wedding, rather than the wedding itself, when she said:

Yeah I thought we might get a bit closer but I don't think that really happened. . . . We'd actually been through a lot of stuff together before we got married, like we had . . . quite a few bad things that we'd gone through together and things that had already strengthened us as a couple so I think we were already really close. We'd gone through a lot of bad stuff as well as good stuff together, so nothing really changed after the wedding.

In general, these participants argued that long-term commitment was more important to them than formalization, and that this commitment existed long before the wedding ceremony.

Conclusions

The nature of our qualitative interviews did not enable us to make generalizations about the impact of formalization on couple relationships or the reactions of others because the sample was too small and unrepresentative of the entire population. However, many participants provided us with insights into this issue by commenting that formalization had made a surprising difference to the way they felt and to the way that others treated them. Especially our same-sex participants noted that they gained some legal rights, respect, and recognition for their relationship that were not there before formalization. Both different-sex and same-sex participants reported that they felt more secure and "settled," and that their families were now more accepting of their long-term partners and included them in family activities. Particularly parents felt that they had created a more secure environment for raising children. Several participants also noted that other people seemed to view formalization as a "rite of passage," indicating a higher level of commitment, a more secure relationship, and a more "adult" lifestyle than cohabitation.

In future research, it would be interesting to see if participants who had large, lavish, or religious weddings were more likely to see "marriage" as transformative in some way. In our interviews, most of the participants who said that formalization made no difference had married in registry offices or in smaller non-religious weddings, and more of these participants were male. However, the very fact that these participants agreed to formalize suggests that they anticipated some gain, such as pleasing their partner or retaining their relationship. Some of our participants (mainly men) reported that they were persuaded to formalize after years of resistance and that they agreed to "marry" in order to maintain a relationship that was important to them.

CHAPTER 6

Conclusions

Introduction

Throughout this book, we have addressed four major questions, locating these within a context of the changing nature of marriage in an era of rising individualism, widespread cohabitation, demands for gender equity in education and employment, opposition to unequal relationships between men and women, and rising levels of relationship instability. First, what prompts so many couples to formalize their relationships after long-term cohabitation? Second, how do couples negotiate this transition with each other as well as with their families and friends? Third, do same-sex couples experience the process of formalization differently from opposite-sex partners? Fourth, does formalization actually alter the couple's identity or relationship in any way, or change the way other people treat them?

To investigate these topics, we have relied on research findings mainly from Australia, Canada, New Zealand, the United Kingdom, and the United States. We have also drawn on our own qualitative interviews from New Zealand, using both the study findings and verbatim comments from our participants to expand on the main themes found in the wider research. Although our purposive sample was not representative of the population of marriage and civil union celebrants or cohabitants, it portrayed a broad range of views in response to the above questions. Generally, our research results reinforced the findings of previous research from other countries but also provided some new insights.

Both our interviews and previous studies suggest that for many people, marriage has retained its symbolic value as a cultural ideal and even become a marker of prestige in an era of declining legal marriage rates and increasing acceptance of same-sex relationships. After years of cohabitation and even after buying a home and raising children, most different-sex couples and a growing number of same-sex couples eventually formalize their relationship. In doing so, they alter their legal and kinship status, enhance their legal rights, but also make public their commitment to each other and celebrate their relationship in a unique way with family and friends.

We have suggested throughout this book that uncovering the patterns in the motives to "marry" and the various ways that couples negotiate the transition from cohabitation to marriage can lead to greater awareness of the increasing impact of individualism, popular culture, and consumerism in everyday life. The book also contributes to a better understanding of changing intimate relationships in the twenty-first century and the growing acceptance of same-sex couples. The research reveals the continuing gendered nature of social relations, including male control of the progression of intimate relationships, the timing of marriage and wedding budgets, and women's greater focus on wedding planning and romance, normality and social acceptance, and the emotional security of a formal union.

This final chapter focuses on six major findings or themes derived from the broader research (including our own) on the transition from cohabitation to marriage. The first refers to the sociological debates we mentioned in Chapter 1 about the "de-traditionalization" and "re-traditionalization" of marriage. The second provides an overview of the different pathways to "marriage" and the gendered circumstances and negotiations surrounding couple decisions to formalize the relationship. The third theme relates to differences between heterosexual couples who choose civil unions and those who choose marriage in a jurisdiction providing two formalization options for heterosexuals. The fourth theme discusses variations in the formalization patterns and the social experiences of participants in same-sex and different-sex relationships. The fifth focuses on reasons for the enhanced personalization and commercial nature of weddings, while the sixth theme discusses whether and why formalization was perceived to be worthwhile by our participants in terms of its personal or social consequences.

Our discussion of these themes is embedded within the larger social, legal, and economic context of the English-speaking countries. This includes an acknowledgement of recent improvements in women's education and earning capacity which make marriage less essential to their economic well-being. It also includes the changing legal trends that blur the differences between cohabitation and marriage and provide greater recognition to same-sex relationships. The conclusions of this book also acknowledge the growth of a more consumer-oriented society, rising levels of economic uncertainty and household debt, and globalizing popular culture over the past few decades. In the next section we discuss the first research theme relating to the de-traditionalization of marriage.

Has Marriage Become "De-Traditionalized"?

In the recent past, marriage blessed by the church and/or state was viewed as a sacrament or legal requirement, the normal way for adults to live and raise children, and the union of two families. At least in theory, marriage helped both men and women to survive and prosper by requiring married partners to share their labour and household resources while providing a secure and socially acceptable environment for sexual expression, child-rearing, and daily living. Since the late twentieth century, however, marriage rates have declined, more couples are cohabiting, more children are born outside of marriage, and separation/divorce rates have increased. Social theorists and researchers have argued that particularly the rise of non-marital cohabitation epitomizes the contemporary trend toward the individualization of society, the rejection of previous pathways to marriage, and the focus on the couple's relationship rather than the union of families.

Sociologists have written about cohabitation as the rejection of standardized models for intimate relationships (Gross 2005: 290), suggesting that young people are abandoning the old social norms and traditions that used to regulate marriage in favour of constructing their own "biographies of love" (Beck and Beck-Gernsheim 1995; Cherlin 2004). By this they mean that couples themselves decide if and when they cohabit, and if and when they marry. Increasingly, they also decide who will marry them, where the ceremony will be held, what they will promise to each other, what they will wear, and how their guests (if there are any) will be entertained, often with very little input from other family members.

From the Victorian era to the 1960s, social norms or regulative traditions expected heterosexual couples to marry before they had sexual relations and certainly before the woman became visibly pregnant. These expectations were enforced in a variety of social ways, including widespread disapproval by family and community members of sex outside marriage, and considerable pressure to marry quickly should a pregnancy occur. Intimate behaviour was also constrained by ineffective contraception that was difficult to access, especially by non-married individuals, as well as illegitimacy laws that punished unmarried mothers and their children, and a gendered labour market that made it difficult for women to support themselves and any children they might have outside marriage.

Over the past fifty years, social life has changed in a number of ways to reduce the need to marry among different-sex couples. Contraception has become more effective and accessible, premarital sexual relations are more socially acceptable, and illegitimacy laws have been repealed. Unmarried mothers can typically receive state income support, although it has become less generous relative to wages in most jurisdictions of the liberal states, and child-care services have become more affordable and more readily available (Baker 2006). Significant changes are also apparent in the labour market, which is much less gendered than it was in the early twentieth century. More domestic services can be purchased from commercial providers, while more women have increased their education and earning capacity. This makes marriage less essential as a means of support for women or a way of maintaining households for both men and women. However, even though more young people delay marriage and some people reject the formalization of their relationships altogether, marriage remains a social ideal and an imagined future for most people (Cherlin 2004; Gross 2005; Kirby 2008; Manning et al. 2007).

Social historians and theorists typically argue that traditions are continually changing but that people seldom reject them outright within a short time span (Gillis 1997; Heelas 1996). In the case of weddings, the research suggests that many couples have dropped some elements of traditional weddings, such as brides promising to obey the groom. Other traditions have been retained, such as walking "down the aisle" even when the couple marries in a park or on a beach, or the couple comprises two lesbian women. Other traditions have been redefined or given new meanings, such as the white wedding dress, which used to be a symbol of bridal virginity and is now simply a traditional wedding dress. Indeed, for many brides this dress has also become more scanty and sexualized, moving even further away from the idea of the virginal bride. We have argued in this book that emphasizing human agency with respect to altering tradition provides a useful point of departure for an examination of the practices used by long-term cohabitants when they transition to marriage or civil unions.

Long-term cohabitants often personalize their weddings, like contemporary weddings in general, creating events that depart from some of the traditional conventions in a number of ways. However, we have argued in this book that creating personalized weddings is not simply a matter of individual choice but that partners are influenced by a number of social, legal, and economic factors shaping their ideas and behaviour. Certainly, the development of personalized weddings has been made possible by the gradual secularization of society, marked by diminishing church attendance and less reliance on religious authority. It has also been made possible by the expansion of registry-office weddings, and especially by the emergence of secular celebrants who in some jurisdictions are permitted to marry couples in a variety of locations.

The personalization of weddings has also been accelerated by the growth of a lucrative wedding industry, which offers a variety of paid services to help couples and families to make their wedding day "special," unique, and memorable, but at a cost. Finally, the increased personalization of weddings is enabled by the current practice for couples to finance their own weddings, a change that has resulted in less parental influence over the style and size of weddings. Where weddings were once an event organized by family members to mark the formation of new family links, they are now much more likely to be organized by the couple (or by the woman and her female relatives), with the assistance of strangers, and to be more centred on the couple's relationship.

Ironically, the de-traditionalization of marriage that is characteristic of personalized weddings co-exists with the preservation of some traditions. These include male marriage proposals in heterosexual weddings, expensive diamond engagement rings, white or cream wedding gowns, the bride entering the ceremony on her father's arm, and a wedding reception providing food, drink, and entertainment. These practices enable couples to simultaneously describe their weddings as having a "personal stamp" but being "pretty traditional." Furthermore, some wedding traditions have been revived with the assistance of intensive advertising by the wedding industry and the recent focus on weddings within popular culture. Sociologists have referred to this pattern as re-traditionalization.

Modern weddings can include traditional symbols of patriarchal and heterosexual marriage even when they involve same-sex couples and individuals with non-traditional values. In fact, several celebrants in our study expressed surprise and annoyance at the traditional wedding practices of so many of their clients, reporting that only a minority seriously attempted to transform the ceremony. Yet the couples themselves often redefined these traditional and patriarchal practices to fit their personal values and preconceptions of a "real" wedding, which often reflect representations from popular culture. And despite their earlier opposition to formalization, some of our participants, both different-sex and same-sex, still expected their friends and families to congratulate them on their eventual decision to marry and to participate enthusiastically in their wedding celebrations. This expectation no doubt reflects their awareness that marriage remains the preferred relationship status of the broader community as well as for most of their parents and older relatives.

As we had expected, the celebrants in our study valued the formalization and celebration of enduring relationships. After all, they would not have chosen this profession if they were not interested in family rituals, rites of passage, or public celebrations. We noted earlier in this book that a female minister of religion in our study commented: "Today's society is so much about living in the *now* and not committing, always having options of doing something else. And so for two people to actually commit themselves to each other is, I think, a really brave thing to do in today's society." We concluded, however, that this "brave thing to do" continues to be the normative practice in all the English-speaking countries, despite anxieties about the implications of greater levels of personal choice in intimate relationships and marriage (Baker and Elizabeth 2012a).

The research suggests that while cohabitation, same-sex unions, and personalized weddings may be transforming marriage in some respects, many long-term cohabitants live in a similar manner to married couples, and most cohabitants who stay together eventually marry. For some couples, the transition from cohabitation to marriage is accompanied by an expectation of greater social recognition of the significance of their partner in their life. Indeed, many participants in our study reported that their partners were accorded a higher level of inclusion in their families following their marriage.

As in the past, weddings remain highly symbolic and gendered, and centre on couples' public commitment to each other, public expectations of reproduction (at least for younger brides and grooms), as well as the union of two families. However, they also continue to be one of the best reasons for a party with family and friends. Marriage is widely viewed as a symbol of enduring relationships among both same-sex and different-sex couples, and among all age groups. Especially parents and older relatives, but also the couple's friends and young children, typically view marriage as a higher level of commitment, and often pressure different-sex cohabiting couples to take what they perceive to be the "next step" in an intimate relationship.

What Are the Prevalent Pathways from Cohabitation to "Marriage"?

Half a century ago, unmarried heterosexual men and women typically lived with their parents when they dated and became "engaged," and only lived together after marriage. Men normally proposed to women, often without any prior discussion between them, and formal engagement could last for years, enabling the couple to strengthen their relationship, save money for their combined future, and spend more time together alone (Baker 2010; Cherlin 2010). Same-sex couples often disguised their sexual preference from family, who continued to pressure them to follow heterosexual lives involving marriage and children.

Now, some of the practices that use to follow marriage actually precede it. For example, many same-sex and different-sex couples cohabit, buy homes, and raise children together before they contemplate formalizing their relationships. In addition, previous research shows that more different-sex couples delay or avoid legal marriage, especially those who are younger, have lower incomes, intend to remain childless, and are not particularly religious (Cherlin 2004; Duncan et al. 2005). Many couples also begin to cohabit without any intention of marrying or formalizing their relationship but simply to enjoy being together and to see how their relationship develops over time. This seems to be something more than "co-residential dating" but less than a trial marriage. This pattern is especially prevalent for same-sex couples for whom legalization has not been possible until recently. However, even couples who see a long-term future together often postpone their wedding until they can find some "valid" reason to marry and until they are certain that they have made the right choice of partner. While many partners separate before making a long-term commitment, most different-sex couples who stay together marry after three to five years of cohabitation. The timing of marriage often coincides with secure employment, money in the bank for their desired wedding, the wish to raise children, and the expectation of a "normal" family life.

In our study, many of the different-sex participants mentioned that they were raised to believe that getting married was the normal adult thing to do. While some reported that they had always wanted to marry, others resisted the pressure because they objected to what they perceived to be the gendered or religious connotations of "traditional" marriage, or because they had been exposed to poor models of marriage or contentious relationships within their own families. Others changed the order of expected life events, such as having a child before marrying, or marrying but remaining childless. A minority of participants argued that formalization was simply unnecessary, implying that neither the church, nor the state, nor their families had the right to interfere in their intimate relationships or personal choices. Nevertheless, they reluctantly agreed to marry in order to please their partner or parents, to gain immigration status or bank loans, or to make their daily lives easier in some other way.

Gay and lesbian participants in various studies report that they were raised with similar assumptions about the normality of marriage and reproduction. However, once they "come out" and live openly with a same-sex partner, they are seldom pressured by parents and older relatives to formalize this relationship, as different-sex couples are encouraged to do. In our study, same-sex couples sometimes decided to formalize their relationship despite family opposition. Some also reported disapproval of their civil union decision from gay and lesbian friends who were antagonistic to the very idea of same-sex marriage, viewing it as heterosexist, patriarchal, unnecessary, or in the case of civil union—"second-class" marriage (Baker and Elizabeth 2012b).

In expressing the reasons for marriage, both the celebrants and cohabitants in our study focused on the importance of making a public commitment and celebrating a successful relationship. This was the same for different-sex and same-sex couples, and for marriages and civil unions, although same-sex participants also emphasized the legal rights and expectations of greater kin acceptance with formalization. However, partners do not always agree about whether or not to formalize, or the timing and nature of their wedding.

Our interviews revealed at least four potential pathways to decisions to formalize: through proposals by one partner, through mutual decisions, through negotiated decisions with partners, and through gradual accommodation of social pressures. The couples where proposals occurred tended to be younger and more conventional than those who made mutual decisions. In different-sex relationships, the marriage proposal typically came from the man, and when it came from the woman, the man often re-proposed before the "engagement" was fully accepted and made public. Among the same-sex participants, the proposal more often came from the older partner even though the initial suggestion to have a civil union often came from the younger partner, who reported more vulnerability without legal rights.

The participants who eventually gave in to the social pressure to marry were varied in their backgrounds, their age, and their social circumstances. However, those involved in prolonged negotiations with partners were usually older and at least one partner had been previously married or involved in other long-term cohabitations. In addition, one partner often opposed marriage as patriarchal, heterosexist, or simply unnecessary, and many of these people seemed to be come from families with divorced or unhappily married parents, or had been divorced themselves. In our study, the opposing partner eventually relented and agreed to marry in order to preserve their relationship or solidify their legal rights as they grew older. However, in several cases, the verbal agreement to marry or have a civil union had not been acted upon at the time of the interview, suggesting that becoming "engaged" could serve as another delaying tactic to formalization.

Why Have Weddings Become So Personalized and Commercial?

We have seen throughout this book that some couples strive to make their weddings into memorable "events" and in doing so, spend months or years planning them and considerable amounts of money. For many cohabiting couples, the wedding no longer serves as a rite of passage to adulthood or the beginning of a new household but instead is seen as an opportunity to celebrate "lasting" relationships and an excuse for a good party. For some, the wedding can also be an occasion for "conspicuous consumption" that involves the provision of lavish food and entertainment to show their guests who they are in terms of their socio-economic status, sexual orientation, and lifestyle preferences. Some couples clearly view their weddings as opportunities to act out their dreams of being a celebrity for the day. Especially in the wedding receptions of different-sex couples, brides and grooms sometimes are ceremoniously "introduced" to their guests by hired masters of ceremony (MCs) in a manner that is similar to television announcers introducing celebrity guests. Several participants in our study mentioned experiencing this in weddings they presided over or attended.

Since the 1970s, wedding practices have been influenced by greater access to credit or borrowed money, which has permitted couples to spend more than they have saved, or more than their families can contribute, on their wedding and honeymoon. Some couples, both different-sex and same-sex, use this as an opportunity to recreate some of the representations of weddings they have seen on television or in popular magazines, as we noted in earlier chapters. They may hire wedding planners, event managers, and marriage celebrants to help them plan and run their weddings, although other couples continue to organize do-it-yourself weddings with help from their families and friends at a minimal cost. Heterosexual women in particular seem to be influenced by advertising from the wedding industry, which profits from expensive engagement and wedding rings, formal wedding dresses and suits, venues for ceremonies and receptions, and costly catering.

In addition, modern weddings continue to be shaped by the opinions, suggestions, and practices of friends, as well as prevalent social ideas about the nature of marriage, sexuality, and gender. Although marriage organizers and celebrants attempt to influence couples in their decisions about what to include in wedding ceremonies, many women have preconceived ideas about the wedding they desire, which draws on childhood fantasies and images from popular culture. For example, some non-religious couples in our study expected to marry in attractive churches without any Bible readings or mention of God, to the dismay of the religious celebrants. Family members also exert influence on cohabiting couples, by pressuring different-sex couples to marry, urging them to invite certain guests, or encouraging them to organize their weddings in particular ways. These different influences suggest that there will be substantial variation in the perceptions of ideal weddings based on gender, sexuality, age, social class, and ethnicity, as well as individual values and experiences.

Is Civil Union the Same as Marriage?

In Canada, same-sex couples have been permitted to marry since 2005, and in the same year same-sex couples in New Zealand and the United Kingdom were allowed to enter civil unions or civil partnerships. As we noted in Chapter 1, many countries extended relationship rights to same-sex couples even earlier, in the form of civil union, civil partnerships, or marriage, while others continue to debate the issue. Legal changes to enable same-sex marriage gave gay and lesbian couples equal rights to different-sex couples, but creating a new category of formalization, like a civil union, typically provides most but not all of the same rights and responsibilities as marriage. In New Zealand at the time of our interviews, same-sex couples who entered civil unions could not adopt children and the validity of their legal relationship was not always accepted in foreign countries.

Our study and the wider research from the United Kingdom and the United States suggest that reasons for entering civil unions, civil relationships, and marriage can be quite similar for same-sex and different-sex participants (Rolfe and Peel 2011; Sassler and Miller 2011; Shipman and Smart 2007; Smart 2008). Both kinds of ceremonies make public an already private commitment and celebrate that relationship with family and friends. Furthermore, our interviews showed less variation than we initially expected in the ceremonies and celebrations for marriage and civil union, including for same-sex and different-sex couples. Most ceremonies were secular and personalized, and many contained traditional elements with gendered or heterosexual symbolism.

Our study contained both different-sex couples who chose civil union over marriage and same-sex couples who could formalize their relationships only through civil union. The number of different-sex couples choosing civil union was admittedly small and were difficult to locate, with only 0.4 percent of heterosexual couples in New Zealand choosing civil unions over marriage (Statistics New Zealand 2011). These participants seemed to believe—rightly or wrongly—that civil union is more inclusive and egalitarian, and less religious, than marriage. In Chapter 2, we argue that civil union is clearly more inclusive but that there is also a long history of civil marriage in the English-speaking countries (including New Zealand), where no religious words are spoken in the ceremony. Although different-sex couples who entered civil unions in New Zealand tend to be younger than the same-sex couples (Statistics New Zealand 2011), the different-sex participants in our study who were entering civil unions also seemed to hold more egalitarian values than those who chose marriage. However, there is no evidence that relationships using civil union as the means of formalization will remain egalitarian over the years in terms of their division of labour or decision-making.

Are Same-Sex and Different-Sex Formalization the Same?

Despite the legal similarities between marriage and civil union/civil partnerships in jurisdictions such as New Zealand, and the fact that ceremonies and celebrations can be indistinguishable, the social context of same-sex and different-sex marriage often varies. Different-sex weddings are generally viewed as normative and celebratory events, although marriage rates are declining as more couples cohabit. However, the formalization of same-sex relationships is surrounded by considerable opposition across a range of disparate communities. In our study, the formalization of same-sex partnerships tended to be characterized by higher levels of tension and unpredictability than are different-sex marriages. Studies from other countries also suggest that it is not unusual for same-sex couples to find that their special day is marred by the unexpected and unexplained absence of key friends and/or family members, or the vituperative comments from guests (Schechter et al. 2008; Smart 2007b). Yet some same-sex couples in our study found, to their surprise, that friends and family members used the occasion of formalization to express their support.

The cultural dominance of marriage and the newness of same-sex formalization mean that same-sex couples who have a civil union or civil partnership typically adopt the language and some of the symbols associated with heterosexual marriage. They may experience romantic proposals by the older partner, talk about being "engaged," wear white dresses or formal suits, and exchange similar vows and wedding rings. However, the recent legalization of civil unions also provides some scope for the creation of unique and personalized ceremonies, a potential that our celebrants suggest is realized more frequently by gay than lesbian couples. Many of the same-sex participants in our study, especially the women, seemed less intent on creating innovative ceremonies and more determined that their wedding would be granted the same respect and social recognition as heterosexual marriage.

Several governments have created legislation that enables same-sex couples to formalize their relationships through civil unions/partnerships, while giving different-sex couples a choice of the type of formalization. In these jurisdictions, heterosexual couples usually choose marriage, but debates in many countries continue about gay rights and the retention of two categories of "marriage." Although social discrimination against gay/lesbian relationships is clearly declining in public polls, it nevertheless continues. Consequently, for many same-sex couples, the formalization of their relationship involves a second "coming out," with all of the accompanying concerns about social acceptance (Baker and Elizabeth 2012c).

Does Formalization Make a Difference?

Previous studies have found that formalization makes a difference to research participants, not only to their own identity and relationship but to the way others treat them (Shipman and Smart 2007). Marriage is still viewed as the normal way to live in adult life. In our study, the long-term cohabitants who proceeded to marriage typically felt that their partner had made a greater commitment to them, giving their relationship a "stronger foundation" and "enhancing the relationship." Getting married seemed to represent both a sign of enhanced dedication but also increased levels of "constraint commitment." Especially women in heterosexual couples and the younger partner in same-sex couples said that marriage or civil union made them feel "more secure," both emotionally and in terms of their kinship and inheritance rights. Several participants living as same-sex couples remarked that formalization makes same-sex relationships more visible to the public by leaving a "paper trail" or historical record of these relationships that had not existed in the past.

In addition, the research shows that recently married participants report that their parents, other relatives, and friends now view their relationship as permanent and therefore more often include their partner in social or family gatherings. Before formalization,

their partner was not always seen as a "family member" and especially gay and lesbian participants report that their parents viewed
their long-term partner as a "friend" or casual "date" rather than
an intimate partner. Our participants also spoke of marriage making things easier for their children at school, and that banks and
mortgage companies were more likely to lend them money to buy
a house if they were married rather than cohabiting. Although a
few of our participants reported that the ceremony made no difference to their relationship or how they were treated by others,
most said that they were surprised that it made so much difference
to the way they felt and to the way others treated them. We need to
keep in mind that many of these couples initially moved in together
without any conscious idea of sharing a future together or having
a trial marriage, but instead they simply wanted to see how the relationship would progress. After marriage, their relationship could
no longer be viewed by others or by themselves as "co-residential
dating" but became an unambiguous long-term commitment.

Our participants also suggested that their wedding provided a
"shared memory" and that they kept photos or videos which they
could view in the future and "look back fondly" at this memorable
event. Some participants spoke of the emotional impact of hearing
their partner making declarations of love in a public place, which
strengthened their feelings for their partner. Others talked about
diminished chances of leaving the relationship now that they had
publicly promised to stay together. They acknowledged that divorce
rates were relatively high, but most participants felt that formalization created additional barriers or constraints to breaking their
relationship, making it more "solid." Although some participants
or their partners initially had been reluctant to marry, the vast majority reported that they now felt it had been the right thing to do.

Conclusions

As more women gain qualifications and enter the workforce, they
become less dependent on male earnings to survive and can more
easily choose to opt out of marriage. With fewer social norms

governing intimate relationships and fewer legal reasons for different-sex couples in particular to marry, intimate partners must
personally negotiate any change to their relationship. However, different-sex and same-sex couples do not always agree about whether or not to marry, when to do it, or the nature of the wedding as
an event. This tends to encourage them to postpone any wedding
preparations until these issues have been clarified, and many relationships end before this happens.

Our research suggests that although women in different-sex relationships and the younger partner in a same-sex relationship are
more likely to initiate the idea of formalization, the actual decision
or the "proposal" is more often made by the male or older partner. This implies that the traditional patriarchal model of decision-
making continues, at least for different-sex couples. In some cases,
agreeing to become "engaged" can be used as a delaying tactic for
those who want to avoid or further postpone formalization. Such
findings are reminiscent of the central role men have played historically in marriage decisions, which used to depend on them gaining adequate resources to establish a new household and support
a family. Furthermore, the timing of marriage and wedding traditions have always varied by social class and ethnicity, with lower
education and income groups marrying and reproducing at younger ages. However, in Chapter 1 we also noted that higher-income
couples are more likely to formalize their relationships and to stay
together than those with fewer resources.

Marriage, in the twenty-first century, is often delayed because
more young people need to gain additional qualifications to find
secure employment and save some money but many also want to
travel and enjoy a higher living standard before marriage and childbearing. Male wages have not always kept up with housing costs
and increased material aspirations, yet men are still expected to
become the primary household earners in labour markets that are
increasingly insecure. Contraception improvements have permitted heterosexual couples to cohabit and experiment with relationships before making any long-term commitment. In addition, high

rates of separation and divorce encourage couples to think carefully about the wisdom of making a long-term commitment. At the same time, we acknowledge that more couples reject any idea that the state or church has the right to compel intimate relationships to take a particular form, even though the state in many jurisdictions views long-term cohabitants to be in a "marriage-like" relationship.

Delayed marriage and higher rates of cohabitation also coincide with the rise of a wedding industry and ideas from popular culture that encourage couples to view their wedding as a life-changing event and a public statement about who they are or who they aspire to become. This encourages more people to believe that they need to acquire considerable resources and make detailed plans before they marry. All these factors suggest that the decision to marry now requires more negotiation between partners and more financial resources than it typically did in past decades.

The research evidence suggests that widespread cohabitation does not really represent the weakening of marriage as a social ideal or anticipated life event, mainly because cohabitation often serves as an implicit if not explicit trial marriage. That being said, many participants in our study, and Lindsay's earlier Australian study (2000), began cohabiting with no immediate intention to marry but rather wanted to see how the relationship would evolve. We might call this pattern of cohabitation "conditional partnership." This form of cohabitation is often entered into with at least some aspiration of a future together if things work out, but nothing as explicit as implied by the notion of a "trial marriage." To understand these relationships in terms of "trial marriage" requires the use of a retrospective lens.

However, we know from the wider research that most young people in the English-speaking countries, including an increasing number of gays and lesbians, still expect to develop a long-term intimate relationship, to marry, and to become parents, even though many now delay marriage until their late twenties or early thirties. Cohabitation as a prelude to marriage has become more prevalent because an increasing number of socio-economic pressures discourage early marriage and child-bearing, while encouraging sexual expression and "constructing one's own biography."

Our research suggests that while cohabitation, same-sex unions, and personalized weddings may be transforming marriage in some respects, marriage continues to be the most prevalent adult living arrangement in the English-speaking countries. As in the past, the wedding as a public commitment remains highly symbolic and still is considered to be one of the best excuses for a celebratory party. Clearly, a diminishing percentage of people in the English-speaking countries see marriage as a sacrament, or even a union between a man and a woman. However, as cohabitation has become the most prevalent pathway to marriage, deciding whether or not to formalize and viewing marriage as the "next step" in the relationship may have become less straightforward than it was in the past.

Methodological Appendix

Study Design

The empirical research presented in this book arose from our mutual interests in the sociology of family and personal life, including Maureen's work on family trends and family policies (Baker 2006, 2009, 2010) and Vivienne's earlier research on cohabitation (Elizabeth 1997, 2000, 2003). Our joint study was based on qualitative interviews completed in 2011 in Auckland, which is New Zealand's largest city (with a population of over one million).

The research design involved two main parts. The first was to interview ten marriage and civil union celebrants as "key informants," because they would be able to provide insights into current wedding practices and trends based on their professional experience. The second was to interview forty individual cohabitants who had lived together for at least three years and had decided to marry or have a civil union, or had already done so. The intention was to focus on the transition from cohabitation to marriage rather than studying cohabitation among those who had no intention to marry or were simply involved in casual cohabitation (or "residential dating"). Previous research has shown that long-term cohabitants are less likely to view cohabitation as part of an explicit pathway to marriage than those cohabiting for shorter periods (Coast 2009; Manning and Smock 2002; Qu 2003). This finding raises interesting questions about what prompts long-term cohabitants to formalize their unions.

We were fortunate to receive research funding from the University of Auckland, which enabled us to hire several sociology students, one to help with the initial review of previous research on cohabitation and the others to carry out most of the interviews. The majority of the interviews were undertaken in the participants' homes by our student interviewers, whom we trained beforehand. All of the interviews were audio-recorded and later transcribed into written scripts by a professional transcriber, whom we hired with the grant money.

The interview sample of cohabitants was intended to be "purposive," which means that we were searching for participants who met a range of social criteria. Among the celebrants, we wanted to interview both males and females, those who were registered by the government to preside over marriages and/or civil unions, celebrants of varying ages and professional experience, those who reported to be heterosexual and gay/lesbian, and ministers of religion as well as independent celebrants who were not affiliated with any particular religious group. We identified potential participants in the Auckland region from celebrant websites, and sent them an email with a formal letter inviting their participation, describing the study, and outlining the ethical protections.

The final sample of ten celebrants reflected many of the characteristics of celebrants living in the Auckland region of New Zealand and included seven women and three men who ranged in age from twenty-eight to sixty-three, with most over forty-five years of age. Most had university degrees in the social sciences or theology and four were ministers of religion, although two of these were also registered as independent celebrants. Five were registered to perform civil unions and marriages, four to perform marriages only, and one to preside only over civil unions.

We asked the celebrants questions about their personal circumstances and training, the patterns and trends they saw in wedding ceremonies and subsequent celebrations, why they thought that many long-term cohabiting couples proceed to formalize their relationships, and the advantages and disadvantages of doing so. Because we used semi-structured in-depth interviews, our participants were able to extend the discussion of issues they felt were important, including describing some of the unique weddings over which they presided. In our analysis, we mapped each celebrant's comments and answers, searched for patterns based on their personal and social characteristics, and extracted illustrative verbatim comments of the key themes that emerged from the ten interviews.

Although the sample of celebrants appears to be small, some of these celebrants had many decades of professional experience, which meant that collectively they had presided over more than 1,500 marriages and hundreds of civil unions.

The second part of the study involved a sample of "long-term" cohabitants who had already decided to formalize their relationships. Again, the sample was intended to be purposive as we wanted to include individuals in gay/lesbian relationships as well as those who were part of different-sex couples. In addition, we wanted to include heterosexuals who chose to have a civil union as well as those who chose marriage. We advertised for these participants within our university and the Auckland community, but also found many participants through the personal networks of our interviewers. The participants who saw our advertisements typically emailed us with their willingness to participate, and we then set up appointments for them to be interviewed in their homes.

In total, we interviewed forty individuals who had been cohabiting with their current partner for at least three years and had already legalized their unions or were planning to do so in the near future. Our final sample included twenty-four females and sixteen males, ranging in age from twenty-eight to sixty-two years. Twenty-seven participants lived in different-sex relationships and thirteen in same-sex relationships. Unexpectedly, thirteen couples volunteered to be interviewed but we interviewed them separately, comparing their stories and viewpoints.

At the time of the interview, thirty-one participants had already married or entered a civil union (some within the past few months and most within the past three years), while nine were "engaged" or about to formalize their relationship. Twenty-three of these participants were planning/ had entered marriage, including six males and seventeen females. Seventeen participants were planning/ had entered civil unions, including five participants who were in different-sex relationships and thirteen who were in same-sex relationships. We deliberately over-represented heterosexual participants who were planning to enter civil unions or had already done so, as there is little research on this very small category of people.

The volunteer nature of the cohabitant sample meant that we were initially reluctant to refuse to interview any potential participants. We eventually curtailed the sample at forty interviews because we were finding no new themes, but we ended up with an over-representation of women and university-educated participants. However, the sample was nevertheless diverse in a number of respects. The participants ranged in age from twenty-eight to sixty-two years, and most were "white" with European ancestry. However, the sample also included participants who were indigenous New Zealanders (Maori), Asian or Eurasian, or immigrants from the United Kingdom, Europe, and North America. Their educational attainment ranged from high school to post-graduate degrees, and their occupations varied from sales clerk to medical doctor. They also differed in their social class background, culture, and religion.

Our interview questions focused on how and why participants came to be cohabiting, how and why they eventually decided to legalize their relationship, and details of their planned or actual weddings. We also asked how their decisions to formalize their relationship were interpreted by friends and family, and whether they anticipated or perceived any change afterward. Although we had a semi-structured interview schedule, which is included at the end of this section, we generally encouraged participants to tell us what they thought was important. In some instances, this led to long personal stories with numerous details on issues that varied from interview to interview. With a small sample, the precise number of participants who made exact comments is relatively meaningless as qualitative research tends to focus on insights rather than percentages. What is more relevant is that some people understand their lives and actions in a particular way, such that they took particular actions.

The analysis of both sets of interviews involved reading and re-reading the transcripts and comparing the comments, themes, or "stories" told by celebrants and cohabitants in different circumstances. In particular, we compared the comments made by men and the women, by the two members of a couple (where both were interviewed), those entering marriage compared to civil union, older and younger participants, and comments made by those in same-sex and different-sex relationships.

Qualitative studies such as ours do not permit researchers to generalize, as their samples are too small and often unrepresentative of the total population. However, the rich and subjective verbatim comments from the celebrants and cohabitants we interviewed deepen our understanding of the patterns and trends found in the wider international research and statistics. More specifically, the comments and stories from our participants provide enlightening details about their personal circumstances and desires, as well as some of the social pressures that influenced their experience of cohabitation and their eventual decision to marry. These stories also provide insights into the reasons for, and details of, the kinds of weddings these men and women have recently experienced or anticipate having, within an environment of rising individualism, consumerism, and the widespread acceptance of unmarried cohabitation as well as same-sex relationships.

Much of the information we now have about cohabitation patterns is derived from official government statistics or other quantitative studies that focus mainly on statistical correlations among variables (such as the associations between cohabitation and youthfulness, low income, and no religious affiliation). We acknowledge that these statistical correlations contribute to our understanding of current patterns of intimate relationships but they can tell us little about personal aspirations, the negotiations between couples, or the social influences that encourage cohabitation, as well as, for some, the formalization of their relationships through marriage or civil union. In this book, we argue that these qualitative interviews can deepen our understanding about why and how these particular individuals and couples negotiate the transition from cohabitation to marriage, which then can be compared to other research findings. In the next section, we present the two interview schedules used in our study.

Interview Schedule for Celebrants

Background Questions
Male/Female
Marital status: Cohabiting/married/civil unioned
Sexual orientation
Highest educational qualification
Occupational background/training
Age
Religious affiliation

Main Questions

1. How long have you been a celebrant?
2. Do you preside over weddings, civil unions, or both?
3. How many weddings or civil unions have you presided over?
4. In your experience as a celebrant, have you seen any trends in the kinds of ceremonies or celebrations people are having?
5. What do you think would be an average cost of these events? Who pays?
6. Why do you think so many people delay or postpone legal marriage these days?
7. Why do you think that couples who have previously cohabited and already have children still have relatively traditional weddings, with symbols of virginity, etc?
8. Do you think that couples generally have realistic expectations of marriage/civil unions?
9. What would you say are the advantages and disadvantages of legalizing relationships?
10. What are the kinds of difficulties or problems do couples encounter during the legalization process?
11. What do you think we should ask individuals and/or couples that are planning to get married/civil unioned or have recently married/civil unioned?

Interview Schedule for Participants in Couple Relationships

Background Information
Male/female
Marital status: Cohabiting/married/civil unioned
Opposite-sex/same-sex relationship
Highest level of education
Occupation
Ethnic/cultural background
Age
Religious affiliation
Have you previously been married/civil unioned? How long did the relationship last?
Have you previously cohabited? How long did the relationship last?
Do you have any children? How old are they?

Main Questions

1. How did you meet your current partner and how did you come to live together?
2. How long have you been living with (or married to) your current partner? (could ask for some details about partner, such as age and occupation)
3. If already married, how long did you cohabit before marriage?
4. When you began living together, was marriage or legalization something you discussed? Did you face any obstacles to marry at that time?
5. What made you decide to legalize your current relationship? Whose idea was it and how did the topic arise? Did one or other of you propose? Has that person initiated important changes in your relationship before?
6. What role did your family and friends play in your decision? How did they react to your news? (search for details of negotiated and gendered behaviour)
    How long will you wait (or did you wait) between the decision to legalize your relationship and the actual ceremony?

7. If a long time, what are (were) you waiting for?
8. What sort of ceremony/wedding are you planning to have (or did you have)?
   Where was/will the ceremony [be] performed? Who presided? What made you choose this celebrant?
9. What did you wear? Were your children involved in the ceremony? What did you promise to your partner?
10. How many guests attended? Were your family there? What roles did your parents play?
    Where was the venue for the celebration?
11. Did you have a honeymoon or go on a trip afterwards?
12. How much, approximately, did the entire event (wedding/party/trip) cost?
13. Did you encounter any difficulties in the lead-up to the ceremony or during the ceremony itself?
14. Do you think that your friends see cohabiting relationships as the same as legal marriage? What about your parents or other relatives?
15. What do you think are the advantages of legal marriage (or civil union)? What do you think are the advantages of cohabitation?
16. Why do you think so many people delay or postpone legal marriage these days?

References

Amato, Paul R., Alan Booth, David R. Johnson, and Stacy J. Rogers. 2007. *Alone Together: How Marriage in America Is Changing*. Cambridge, MA: Harvard University Press.

Ambert, Anne-Marie. 2005. "Same-Sex Couples and Same-Sex-Parent Families: Relationships, Parenting and Issues of Marriage." Vanier Institute of the Family. http://www.vanierinstitute.ca/include/get.php?nodeid=1150.

Australian Bureau of Statistics. 2007. *Marriages, Australia, 2006*. www.abs.gov.au/AUSSTATS/.

———. 2008. *Births, Australia, 2007*. http://www.abs.gov.au/AUSSTATS/abs@.nsf/mf.3301.0.

Australian Institute of Family Studies. 2008. *Family Facts and Figures*. http://www.aifs.gov.au/institute/info/charts/cohabitation/index.html.

Bainham, Andrew. 2006. "Status Anxiety: The Rush for Family Recognition." In *Kinship Matters*, edited by Fatemeh Ebtehaj, Bridget Lindley, and Martin Richards, 47–65. Oxford: Hart Publishing.

Baker, Maureen. 2001. *Families, Labour and Love: Family Diversity in a Changing World*. Sydney and Vancouver: Allen & Unwin and University of British Columbia Press.

———. 2006. *Restructuring Family Policies: Convergences and Divergences*. Toronto: University of Toronto Press.

———. 2009. *Families: Changing Trends in Canada*, 6th edn. Toronto: McGraw-Hill Ryerson.

———. 2010. *Choices and Constraints in Family Life*, 2nd edn. Toronto: Oxford University Press.

Baker, Maureen, and Vivienne Elizabeth. 2012a. "'A Brave Thing to Do' or a Normative Practice? Marriage after Long-Term Cohabitation." *Journal of Sociology*. First published online 17 October.

———. 2012b. "Negotiating 'Marriage': Comparing Same-Sex and Different-Sex Cohabiting Couples." *New Zealand Sociology* 27 (2): 1–20.

———. 2012c. "Second-Class Marriage? Civil Union in New Zealand." *Journal of Comparative Family Studies* 43 (5): 633–45.

———. 2011. "Sliding or Deciding? Negotiating the Transition from Cohabitation to Marriage/Civil Union." Refereed paper for the Australian Sociological Association, University of Newcastle, November 29–December 1.

Barber, Jennifer S., and William G. Axinn. 1998. "The Impact of Parental Pressure for Grandchildren on Young People's Entry into Cohabitation and Marriage." *Population Studies* 52 (2): 129–44.

Baxter, Janeen. 2002. "Patterns of Change and Stability in the Gender Division of Household Labour in Australia, 1986–1997." *Journal of Sociology* 38 (4): 399–424.

———, and Michael Bittman. 1995. "Measuring Time Spent on Housework: A Comparison of Two Approaches." *Australian Journal of Social Research* 1 (1): 21–46.

———, Michele Haynes, and Belinda Hewitt. 2010. "Pathways into Marriage: Cohabitation and the Domestic Division of Labor." *Journal of Family Issues* 31 (11): 1509–29.

Beck, Ulrich, and Beck-Gernsheim, Elisabeth 1995. *The Normal Chaos of Love*. Cambridge, UK: Polity Press.

Beck-Gernsheim, Elisabeth. 2002. *Reinventing the Family: In Search of New Lifestyles*. Cambridge, UK: Polity Press.

Beeby, Dean. 2006. "Legalize Polygamy, Federal Study Urges." *GlobeandMail.com*. 13 January.

Berrington, Ann. 2001. "Entry into Parenthood and the Outcomes of Cohabiting Partnerships in Britain." *Journal of Marriage and Family* 63 (1):80–96.

Bibby, Reginald. 2004. *The Future Families Project: A Survey of Canadian Hopes and Dreams*. http://www.vifamily.ca.

Black, Dan, et al. 2000. "Demographics of the Gay and Lesbian Population in the United States: Evidence from Available Systematic Data Sources." *Demography* 37: 139–54.

Blakely, Kristin. 2008. "Busy Brides and the Business of Family Life." *Journal of Family Issues* 29: 639–62.

Boden, Sharon. 2001. "'Superbrides': Wedding Consumer Culture and the Construction of Bridal Identity." *Sociological Research Online* 6 (1). www.socresonline.org.uk.

———. 2003. *Consumerism, Romance and the Wedding Experience*. New York: Palgrave Macmillan.

Bogle, Kathleen A. 2008. *Hooking Up: Sex, Dating, and Relationships on Campus*. New York: New York University Press.

Booth, Alan, and Anne C. Crouter, eds. 2002. *Just Living Together: Implications of Cohabitation on Families, Children, and Social Policy*. Hillside, NJ: Erlbaum Associates.

Buchler, Sandra, Janeen Baxter, Michele Haynes, and Mark Western. 2008. "The Social and Demographic Characteristics of Cohabiters in Australia: Towards a Typology of Cohabiting Couples." Presented at the 10th Australian Institute of Family Studies Conference, 9–11 July, Melbourne.

Butler, Judith. 1990. *Gender Trouble: Feminism and the Subversion of Identity*. New York: Routledge, Chapman and Hall.

Byrd, Stephanie Ellen. 2009. "The Social Construction of Marital Commitment." *Journal of Marriage and Family* 71 (May): 318–36.

Canadian Wedding Guide. 2012. "Average Cost of a Canadian Wedding." www.mycanadian-wedding.com.

Carmichael, Gordon A., and Andrea Whittaker. 2007a. "Forming Relationships in Australia: Qualitative Insights into a Process Important to Human Wellbeing." *Journal of Population Research* 24 (1): 23–49.

———. 2007b. "Living Together in Australia: Qualitative Insights into a Complex Phenomenon." *Journal of Family Studies* 13 (2): 202.

Cherlin, Andrew J. 2004. "The Deinstitutionalization of American Marriage." *Journal of Marriage and Family* 66 (4): 848–61.

———. 2010. *The Marriage-Go-Round: The State of Marriage and the Family in America Today*. New York: Knopf Doubleday.

Coast, Ernestina. 2009. "Currently Cohabiting: Relationship Attitudes, Expectations and Outcomes." In *Fertility, Living Arrangements Care and Mobility: Understanding Population Trends and Processes*, edited by John Stillwell, Ernestina Coast, and Dylan Kneale. Dordrecht: Springer.

Coontz, Stephanie. 2005. *Marriage, A History: From Obedience to Intimacy, or How Love Conquered Marriage*. New York: Penguin.

Currie, Dawn. 1993. "Here Comes the Bride: The Making of a Modern Traditional Wedding in Western Culture." *Journal of Comparative Family Studies* 24 (3): 403–21.

Daly, Mary, and Katherine Rake. 2003. *Gender and the Welfare State*. Cambridge, UK: Polity Press.

Davis, Shannon N., Theodore N. Greenstein, and Jennifer P. Marks. 2007. "Effects of Union Type on Division of Household Labor," *Journal of Family Issues* 28 (9): 1246–72.

de Vaus, David. 2004. *Diversity and Change in Australian Families: Statistical Profiles*. Melbourne: Australian Institute of Family Studies.

———, Lixia Qu, and Ruth Weston. 2005. "The Disappearing Link between Premarital Cohabitation and Subsequent Marital Stability, 1970–2001." *Journal of Population Research* 22: 99–118.

Dempsey, Ken, and David de Vaus. 2004. "Who Cohabits in 2001? The Significance of Age, Gender, Religion and Ethnicity." *Journal of Sociology* 40 (2), 157–78.

Dranoff, Linda Silver. 1977. *Women in Canadian Life*. Toronto: Fitzhenry & Whiteside.

Duncan, Simon, Anne Barlow, and Grace James. 2005. "Why Don't They Marry?: Cohabitation, Commitment and DIY Marriage." *Child and Family Law Quarterly* 17: 383–98.

Dunne, Gillian A. 1997. *Lesbian Lifestyles: Women's Work and the Politics of Sexuality.* Toronto: University of Toronto Press.

Duvander, Ann-Zofie E. 1999. "The Transition From Cohabitation to Marriage: A Longitudinal Study of the Propensity to Marry in Sweden in the Early 1990s." *Journal of Family Issues* 20 (5): 698–717.

Edin, Kathryn, and Maria J. Kefalas. 2005. *Promises I Can Keep: Why Poor Women Put Motherhood before Marriage.* Berkeley: University of California Press.

———, and Joanna M. Reed. 2005. "Why Don't They Just Get Married?: Barriers to Marriage among the Disadvantaged." *Marriage and Child Wellbeing* 15 (2): 117–36.

Einarsdottir, Anna. 2011. "'Marriage' and the Personal Life of Same-Sex Couples." In *Sociology of Personal Life*, edited by Vanessa May, 48–58. Basingstoke: Palgrave Macmillan.

Elizabeth, Vivienne. 1997. "Something Old, Something Borrowed, Something New: Heterosexual Cohabitation as Marriage Resistance? A Feminist Deconstruction." PhD thesis, Department of Sociology, University of Canterbury, Christchurch, New Zealand.

———. 2000. "Cohabitation, Marriage, and the Unruly Consequences of 'Difference'." *Gender and Society* 14 (1): 87–100.

———. 2001. "Sexual Citizenship in Aotearoa/New Zealand: A Case Study of the Property (Relationship) Bill." Paper presented at the Annual TASA (Australian Sociological Association) Conference, University of Sydney, Sydney. 16–18 December.

———. 2003. "To Marry, or Not to Marry: That Is the Question." *Feminism and Psychology* 13: 427–31.

———, and Maureen Baker. 2010. "Negotiating the Transition from Cohabitation to 'Marriage.'" Refereed Paper for "Social Causes, Private Lives." The Australian Sociological Association, Macquarie University. Sydney. 6–9 December.

Ellison, Christopher G., Amy M. Burdette, and Norval D. Glenn. 2011. "Praying for Mr. Right?: Religion, Family Background and Marital Expectations among College Women." *Journal of Family Issues* 32 (7): 906–31.

Ermisch, John, and Marco Francesconi. 2000. "Cohabitation in Great Britain: Not for Long, But Here to Stay." *Journal of the Royal Statistical Society: Series A (Statistics in Society)* 163 (2): 153–71.

Fairbairn, Catherine. 2011. *"Common-Law Marriage" and Cohabitation.* London: UK Parliament, Home Affairs Section.

Fletcher, Ronald. 1973. *The Family and Marriage in Britain.* Harmondsworth: Penguin.

Funder, Kathleen. 1996. *Remaking Families: Adaptation of Parents and Children to Divorce.* Melbourne: Australian Institute of Family Studies.

——— and Margaret Harrison. 1993. "Drawing a Longbow on Marriage and Divorce." In *Settling Down: Pathways of Parents after Divorce*, edited by Margaret Harrison, Kathleen Funder, and Ruth Weston, 13–32. Melbourne: Australian Institute of Family Studies.

Geller, Jaclyn. 2001. *Here Comes the Bride: Women, Weddings and the Marriage Mystique.* New York: Four Walls Eight Windows.

Giddens, Anthony. 1992. *The Transformation of Intimacy: Sexuality, Love and Eroticism in Modern Societies.* Cambridge, UK: Polity Press.

Gillis, John R. 1997. *A World of Their Own Making: Myth, Ritual, and the Quest for Family Values.* New York: Basic Books.

Goffman, Erving. 1959. *The Presentation of Self in Everyday Life.* Garden City, NY: Doubleday Anchor.

Greenwood, Gaye A. 1999. "Dissolution of Marriage: Public Policy and 'The Family-Apart'." MA Thesis, School of Social Policy and Social Work, Massey University at Aukland.

Gross, Neil. 2005. "The Detraditionalization of Intimacy Reconsidered." *Sociological Theory* 23 (3): 286–311.

Hamilton, Laura, Claudia Geist, and Brian Powell. 2011. "Marital Name Change as a Window into Gender Attitudes." *Gender and Society* 25 (April): 145–75.

Haskey, John. 1999. "Cohabitational and Marital Histories of Adults in Great Britain." *Population Studies* 96: 13–24.

Heelas, Paul. "Introduction: Detraditionalization and Its Rivals." In *Detraditionalization: Critical Reflections on Authority and Identity*, edited by Paul Heelas, Scott Lash, and Paul Morris, 1–20. Oxford: Blackwell, 1996.

Heuveline, Patrick, and Jeffrey M. Timberlake. 2004. "The Role of Cohabitation in Family Formation: The United States in Comparative Perspective." *Journal of Marriage and the Family* 66 (5): 1214–30.

Hewitt, Belinda, and David de Vaus. 2009. "Change in the Association between Premarital Cohabitation and Separation, Australia 1945–2000." *Journal of Marriage and Family* 71 (2): 353–61.

———, and Janeen Baxter. 2012. "Who Gets Married in Australia?: The Characteristics Associated with a Transition into First Marriage 2001–6." *Journal of Sociology* 48 (1): 43–61.

Hibbs, Mary, Chris Barton, and Joanne Beswick. 2001. "Why Marry?: Perceptions of the Affianced." *Family Law Journal* 31 (March): 197–207.

Hoffman, Saul D., and E. Michael Foster. 1997. "Economic Correlates of Nonmarital Childbearing among Adult Women." *Family Planning Perspectives* 29 (3): 137–40.

Huang, Penelope M., Pamela J. Smock, Wendy D. Manning, and Cara A. Bergstrom-Lynch. 2011. "He Says, She Says: Gender and Cohabitation." *Journal of Family Issues* 32 (7): 876–905.

Humble, Áine M. 2009. "The Second Time 'Round: Gender Construction in Remarried Couples' Wedding Planning." *Journal of Divorce and Remarriage* 50 (4): 260–81.

———, Anisa M. Zvonkovic, and Alexis J. Walker. 2008. "'The Royal We': Gender Ideology, Display and Assessment in Wedding Work." *Journal of Family Issues* 29: 3–25.

Husbands, Lucy. 2006. *Laboured Romance: Wedding Tourism in Aotearoa New Zealand*. MA Thesis, Department of Sociology, University of Auckland, New Zealand.

Inglis, B. D. 2007. *New Zealand Family Law in the 21st Century*. Wellington, NZ: Thomson Brookers.

Ingraham, Chrys. 2008. *White Weddings: Romancing Heterosexuality in Popular Culture*, 2nd edn. New York: Routledge.

Jamieson, Lynn, Michael Anderson, David McCrone, Franch Bechhofer, Robert Stewart, and Yaojun Li. 2002. "Cohabitation and Commitment: Partnership Plans of Young Men and Women." *The Sociological Review* 50 (3): 356–77.

Johnston, Lynda. 2006. "'I Do Down-Under': Naturalizing Landscapes and Love through Wedding Tourism in New Zealand." *ACME: An International E-Journal for Critical Geographies* 5 (2): 191–208.

Jowett, Adam, and Elizabeth Peel. 2010. "'Seismic Cultural Change?': British Media Representations of Same-Sex 'Marriage'." *Women's Studies International Forum* 33: 206–14.

Kefalas, Maria J., Frank F. Furstenberg, Patrick J. Carr, and Laura Napolitano. 2011. "'Marriage is More than Being Together': The Meaning of Marriage for Young Adults." *Journal of Family Issues* 32 (7): 845–75.

Kennedy, Sheela, and Larry Bumpass. 2008. "Cohabitation and Children's Living Arrangements: New Estimates from the United States." *Demographic Research* 19: 1663–92.

Kerr, Don, Melissa Moyser, and Roderic Beaujot. 2006. "Marriage and Cohabitation: Demographic and Socioeconomic Differences in Quebec and Canada." *Canadian Studies in Population* 33 (1): 83–117.

Kimmel, Michael S. 2008. *The Gendered Society.* New York: Oxford University Press.

Kirby, Emma. 2008. "Coexisting Detraditionalization and Retraditionalization in Young White Middle Class Women's Marriage Attitudes." Paper presented at the Re-imagining Sociology: Annual TASA Conference, University of Melbourne, Melbourne. 5–8 December.

Kurdeck, Lawrence A. 1998. "Relationship Outcomes and Their Predictors: Longitudinal Evidence from Heterosexual Married, Gay Cohabiting and Lesbian Cohabiting Couples." *Journal of Marriage and the Family* 60: 553–68.

———. 2001. "Differences between Heterosexual-Nonparent Couples and Gay, Lesbian and Heterosexual-Parent Couples." *Journal of Family Issues* 22: 728–55.

Lauer, Sean, and Carrie Yodanis. 2010. "The Deinstitutionalization of Marriage Revisited: A New Institutional Approach to Marriage." *Journal of Family Theory and Review* 2 (1): 58–72.

Le Bourdais, Céline, and Evelyne Lapierre-Adamcyk. 2004. "Changes in Conjugal Life in Canada: Is Cohabitation Progressively Replacing Marriage?" *Journal of Marriage and Family* 66 (November): 929–42.

Lewis, Charlie, Amalia Papacosta, and Jo Warin. 2002. *Cohabitation, Separation and Fatherhood.* York: Foundation for Family Policy Studies Centre.

Lewis, Jane. 1999. "Marriage and Cohabitation and the Nature of Commitment." *Child and Family Law Quarterly* 11 (4): 355–63.

———. 2001. *The End of Marriage?* Cheltenham: Edward Elgar.

Lichter, Daniel T., and Zhenchao Qian. 2008. "Serial Cohabitation and the Marital Life Course." *Journal of Marriage and Family* 70 (4): 861–78.

———, Zhenchao Qian, and Leanna M. Mellot. 2006. "Marriage or Dissolution? Union Transitions Among Poor Cohabiting Women." *Demography* 43 (2): 223–40.

Liefbroer, Aart C., and Edith Dourleijn. 2006. "Unmarried Cohabitation and Union Stability: Testing the Role of Diffusion Using Data from 16 European Countries." *Demography* 43 (2): 203–21.

Lindsay, Jo. 2000. "An Ambiguous Commitment: Moving in to a Cohabiting Relationship." *Journal of Family Studies* 6 (1): 120–34.

McLaughlin, Diane K., and Daniel T. Lichter. 1997. "Poverty and the Marital Behavior of Young Women." *Journal of Marriage and the Family* 59: 589.

McNair, Ruth, Deborah Dempsey, Sarah Wise, and Amaryll Perlesz. 2002. "Lesbian Parenting: Issues, Strengths and Challenges." *Family Matters* 63: 40–49.

Manning, Wendy, Jessica A. Cohen, and Pamela J. Smock. 2011. "The Role of Romantic Partners, Family, and Peer Networks in Dating Couples' Views About Cohabitation." *Journal of Adolescent Research* 26 (1): 115–49.

———, Monica A. Longmore, and Peggy C. Giordano. 2007. "The Changing Institution of Marriage: Adolescents' Expectations to Cohabit and Marry." *Journal of Marriage and Family* 69: 559–75.

Manning, Wendy D., and Pamela J. Smock. 2002. "First Comes Cohabitation and Then Comes Marriage? A Research Note." *Journal of Family Issues* 23 (8): 1065–87.

Matheson, Clare. 2006. "Wedding Industry in the Pink." BBC Business News, 14 February.

May, Vanessa, ed. 2011. *Sociology of Personal Life.* Basingstoke, UK: Palgrave Macmillan.

McCarthy, Jane Ribberns, Rosalind Edwards, and Val Gillies. 2003. *Making Families: Moral Tales of Parenting and Step-Parenting.* London: Sociology Press.

Moore, Oliver. 2003. "Bush Wants to 'Codify' Heterosexual Unions." *Globe and Mail.* 31 July.

Nayak, Anoop, and Mary Jane Kehily. 2008. *Gender, Youth and Culture: Young Masculinities and Femininities.* Basingstoke, UK: Palgrave Macmillan.

New Zealand Department of Internal Affairs. 2011. "Becoming a Marriage Celebrant." www. dia.govt.nz. With follow-up email from Ross McPherson, 12 April 2011.

OECD. 2007. *A Synthesis of Findings for OECD Countries*. Vol. 5 of *Babies and Bosses: Reconciling Work and Family Life*. www/oecd.org/els/social/family. Paris: OECD.

———. 2009. *Society at a Glance 2009*. Paris: OECD.

Ontario Government. 2012. "Getting Married in Ontario." Toronto: Queen's Printer.

Oswald, Ramona Faith, and Elizabeth A. Suter. 2004. "Heterosexist Inclusion and Exclusion during Ritual: A 'Straight versus Gay' Comparison." *Journal of Family Issues* 25: 881–99.

Otnes, Cele, and Elizabeth H. Pleck. 2003. *Cinderella Dreams: The Allure of the Lavish Wedding*. Berkeley, CA: University of California Press.

Patterson, Charlotte J. 2000. "Family Relationships of Lesbians and Gay Men," *Journal of Marriage and the Family* 62: 1052–69.

Pongracz, Marietta, and Zsolt Spéder. 2008. "Attitudes Towards Forms of Partnership." In *Family Change*, Vol. 1 of *People, Population Change and Policies*, edited by Charlotte Höhn, Avramov Dragana, and Irena E. Kotowska. New York: Springer.

Porter, Meredith, Wendy D. Manning, and Pamela J. Smock. 2004. "Cohabitors' Prerequisites for Marriage: Individual, Relationship, and Sociocultural Influences." Bowling Green State University, Centre for Family and Demographic Research. Research Paper #2004-09.

Pryor, Jan, and Josie Roberts. 2005. "What is Commitment?: How Married and Cohabiting Parents Talk about Their Relationships." *Family Matters* 71 (Winter): 24–31.

Qu, Lixia. 2003. "Expectations of Marriage Among Cohabiting Couples." *Family Matters* 64: 36–39.

———, and Ruth Weston. 2008a. "Family Statistics and Trends: Attitudes Towards Marriage and Cohabitation." *Family Relationship Quarterly* 8: 5–10.

———. 2008b. "Snapshot of Family Relationships." *Family Matters*. Published by the Australian Institute of Family Studies. May 2008.

———, Ruth Weston, and David de Vaus. 2009. "Cohabitation and Beyond: The Contribution of Each Partner's Relationship Satisfaction and Fertility Aspirations to Pathways of Cohabiting Couples." *Journal of Comparative Family Studies* 40 (4): 587–601.

Ravanera, Zenaida R., and Fernando Rajulton. 2007. "Changes in Economic Status and Timing of Marriage of Young Canadians." *Canadian Studies in Population* 34 (1): 49–67.

Rhoades, Galena Kline, Scott M. Stanley, and Howard J. Markman. 2009. "Pre-engagement Cohabitation and Gender Asymmetry in Marital Commitment." *Journal of Family Psychology,* 23 (1): 107–11.

———. 2010. "Should I Stay or Should I Go?: Predicting Dating Relationship Stability from Four Aspects of Commitment." *Journal of Family Psychology* 24: 543–50.

Richters, Juliet and Chris Rissel. 2005. *Doing It Down Under*. Sydney: Allen and Unwin.

Rolfe, Alison, and Elizabeth Peel. 2011. "'It's a Double-Edged Thing': The Paradox of Civil Partnership and Why Some Couples Are Choosing Not to Have One." *Feminism and Psychology* 21 (3): 317–35.

Rothblum, Esther D. 2005. "Same-Sex Marriages and Legalized Relationships: I Do, or Do I?" *Journal of GLBT Family Studies* 1 (1): 21–31.

Sarantakos, Sotirios. 1998. "Sex and Power in Same-Sex Couples." *Australian Journal of Social Issues* 33 (1): 17–36.

Sassler, Sharon, and Amanda Miller. 2011. "Waiting To Be Asked: Gender, Power and Relationship Progression among Cohabiting Couples." *Journal of Family Issues* 32 (4): 482–506.

Scanzoni, John. 1982. *Sexual Bargaining: Power Politics in American Marriage*, 2nd edn. Chicago: University of Chicago Press.

Schecter, Ellen, Allison J. Tracy, Konjit V. Page, and Gloria Luong. 2008. "'Shall We Marry?':

Legal Marriage as a Commitment Event in Same-Sex Relationships." *Journal of Homosexuality* 54 (4): 400–22.

Scott, Jacqueline. 2006. *Family and Gender Roles: How Attitudes Are Changing*. GeNet Working Paper No. 21. Cambridge, UK: University of Cambridge.

Shechory, Mally, and Riva Ziv. 2007. "Relationships between Gender Role Attitudes, Role Division, and Perception of Equity between Heterosexual, Gay and Lesbian Couples." *Sex Roles* 56 (9–10): 629–38.

Shipman, Beccy, and Carol Smart. 2007. "'It's Made a Huge Difference': Recognition, Rights and the Personal Significance of Civil Partnership." *Sociological Research Online* 12 (1).

Shulman, Julie L., Gabrielle Gotta, and Robert-Jay Green. 2012. "Will Marriage Matter?: Effects of Marriage Anticipated by Same-Sex Couples." *Journal of Family Issues* 33 (2): 158–81.

Smart, Carol. 2005. "Textures of Family Life: Further Thoughts on Change and Commitment." *Journal of Social Policy* 34 (4): 541–56.

——. 2007a. *Personal Life*. Cambridge, UK: Polity Press.

——. 2007b. "Same Sex Couples and Marriage: Negotiating Relational Landscapes with Families and Friends." *The Sociological Review* 55 (4): 671–86.

——. 2008. "'Can I Be Bridesmaid?': Combining the Personal and Political in Same-Sex Weddings." *Sexualities* 11 (6): 763–78.

——. 2009. "Family Secrets: Law and Understandings of Openness in Everyday Relationships." *Journal of Social Policy* 38 (4): 551–67.

——. 2011. "Close Relationships and Personal Life." In *The Sociology of Personal Life*, edited by Vanessa May, 35–47. Balingstoke, UK: Palgrave Macmillan.

——, and Pippa Stevens. 2000. *Cohabiting Parents' Experiences of Relationships and Separation*. York: Foundation for Family Policy Studies Centre.

Smock, Pamela J., and Wendy D. Manning. 1997. "Cohabiting Partners' Economic Circumstances and Marriage." *Demography* 34: 331–41.

——, Wendy D. Manning, and Meredith Porter. 2005. "'Everything's There Except Money': How Money Shapes Decisions to Marry among Cohabitors." *Journal of Marriage and Family* 67 (3): 680–96.

Smyth, Bruce, ed. 2004. *Parent–Child Contact and Post-Separation Parenting Arrangements*. Research Report #9. Melbourne: Australian Institute of Family Studies.

Sniezek, Tamara. 2005. "Is it Our Day or the Bride's Day? The Division of Wedding Labour and its Meaning for Couples." *Qualitative Sociology* 28 (3): 215–34.

Solomon, Sondra E., Esther D. Rothblum, and Kimberly F. Balsam. 2005. "Money, Housework, Sex and Conflict: Same-Sex Couples in Civil Unions, Those Not in Civil Unions, and Heterosexual Married Siblings." *Sex Roles* 52 (9–10): 561–75.

Stanley, Scott M., Galena Kline Rhoades, and Howard J. Markman. 2006. "Sliding Versus Deciding: Inertia and the Premarital Cohabitation Effect." *Family Relations* 55 (October): 499–509.

Statistics Canada. 2002. "Changing Conjugal Life in Canada." *The Daily*. 11 July.

——. 2003. "Marriages." *The Daily*. 2 June.

——. 2007a. *Family Portrait: Continuity and Change in Canadian Families and Households in 2006*. www12.statcan.ca/english/census06.

——. 2007b. *The Daily*. 12 September.

——. 2008. "Live Births, by Geography—Marital Status of Mother," Table 2.5. http://www.statcan.gc.ca/pub/84f0210x/2006000/5201681-eng.htm.

——. 2012. "2011 Census of Population: Families, Households, Marital Status, Structural Type of Dwelling, Collectives." *The Daily*. 19 September.

Statistics New Zealand. 2001. "Marriage and Divorce in New Zealand: Key Statistics."

——. 2002. *2001 Census: Families and Households*. http://www.stats.govt.nz/Census/2001-census-data/2001-census-families-and-households.aspx.

———. 2010a. "Characteristics of Same-Sex Couples in New Zealand."

———. 2010b. "Demographic Trends 2010."

———. 2010c. *Wedding Tourism: 1980–2009.*

———. 2011. "Marriages, Civil Unions and Divorces: Year Ending December 2009." www.stats.govt.nz.

———. 2012. *Demographic Trends: 2011.*

Steele, Fiona, Constantinos Kallis, Harvey Goldstein, and Heather Joshi. 2005. "The Relationship between Childbearing and Transitions from Marriage and Cohabitation in Britain." *Demography* 42 (4): 647–73.

Sullivan, Andrew, ed. 2004. *Same-Sex Marriage Pro and Con: A Reader*, rev. edn. New York: Vintage.

Tombaugh, Alissa. 2009. "Pretty Dresses and Privilege: Gender and Heteronormativity in Weddings." *Sociological Insight* 1: 106–23.

UK Office of National Statistics. 2010. *Estimating the Cohabiting Population, 2007.* www.ons.gov.uk.

US Bureau of the Census. 2011a. "Median Age at First Marriage, 1890 to 2010." www.census.gov.

US Bureau of the Census. 2011b. "Same-Sex Couple Households." www.census.gov.

Vanier Institute of the Family. 1994. *Profiling Canada's Families.*

———. 2000. *Profiling Canada's Families II.*

———. 2004. *Profiling Canada's Families III.* http://www.vanierinstitute.ca/include/get.php?nodeid=53.

———. 2007. *Family Facts.* http://www.vifamily.ca/library/facts/ facts.html.

———. 2008. "Fertility Intentions: If, When and How Many?" *Fascinating Families.* http://www.vanierinstitute.ca/include/get.php?nodeid=813.

———. 2011. "Marriage Rate Continues to Drop." *Fascinating Families* 40. 28 September. http://www.vanierinstitute.ca/modules/news/newsitem.php?ItemId=82#.UaZVG9iQmcM.

———. 2012. "Births and Babies in 2009." *Just the Facts.* 18 April. http://www.vanierinstitute.ca/modules/news/newsitem.php?ItemId=431#.UaZVaNiQmcM.

Veblen, Thorstein. 1899 (1953). *The Theory of the Leisure Class: An Economic Study of Institutions.* New York: Mentor.

Waaldijik, Kees. 2001. "Small Change: How the Road to Same-Sex Marriage Got Paved in the Netherlands." in *Legal Recognition of Same-Sex Relationships: A Study of National, European and International Law,* edited by Robert Wintemute and Mads Tønnessen Andenaes, 437–64. Oxford: Hart Publishing.

Wallace, Carol. 2004. *All Dressed in White: The Irresistible Rise of the American Wedding.* New York: Penguin.

Wedding Report, The. 2012. "Cost of Wedding." www.theweddingreport.com.

Weeks, Jeffrey. 2002. "Elective Families: Lesbian and Gay Life Experiments." In *Analysing Families: Morality and Rationality in Policy and Practice,* edited by Alan Carling, Simon Duncan, and Rosalind Edwards, 218–28. London: Routledge.

———. 2007. *The World We Have Won: The Remaking of Erotic and Intimate Life.* Oxford: Routledge.

———, Brian Heaphy, and Catherine Donovan. 2001. *Same-Sex Intimacies: Families of Choice and Other Life Experiments.* London: Routledge.

West, Candace, and Don H. Zimmerman. 1987. "Doing Gender." *Gender and Society* 1 (2): 125–51.

Weston, Kath. 1991. *Families We Choose: Lesbians, Gays, Kinship.* New York: Columbia University Press.

Williams, Matt. 2012. "New York's Gay Marriage Industry is Booming One Year After First Weddings." *The Guardian.* 24 July.

Willoughby, Brian J., Jason S. Carroll, Jennifer M. Vitas, and Lauren M. Hill. 2012. "'When Are You Getting Married?': The Intergenerational Transmission of Attitudes Regarding Marital Timing and Marital Importance." *Journal of Family Issues* 33 (2): 223–45.

Wilson, Sue. 2009. "Partnering, Cohabitation and Marriage." In *Families: Changing Trends in Canada*, 6th edn, edited by Maureen Baker, 49–67. Toronto: McGraw-Hill Ryerson.

Wu, Lawrence L. 2008. "Cohort Estimates of Nonmarital Fertility for U.S. Women." *Demography* 45 (1): 193–207.

Wu, Zheng. 1999. "Premarital Cohabitation and the Timing of First Marriage." *The Canadian Review of Sociology and Anthropology* 36: 109–27.

———. 2000. *Cohabitation: An Alternative Form of Family Living*. Toronto: Oxford University Press.

——— and T.R. Balakrishnan. 1995. "Dissolution of Premarital Cohabitation in Canada." *Demography* 32 (4): 521–532.

——— and Michael S. Pollard. 2000. "Economic Circumstances and the Stability of Nonmarital Cohabitation." *Journal of Family Issues* 21 (3): 303–28.

——— and Christoph Schimmele. 2009. "Divorce and Repartnering." In *Families: Changing Trends in Canada*, edited by Maureen Baker, 154–78. Toronto: McGraw-Hill Ryerson.

Index